New Thought

New Thought

A Practical Spirituality

edited by Mary Manin Morrissey

Jeremy P. Tarcher/Putnam
a member of Penguin Group (USA) Inc.
New York

Most Tarcher/Putnam books are available at special quantity discounts
for bulk purchase for sales promotions, premiums, fund-raising, and
educational needs. Special books or book excerpts also can be created
to fit specific needs. For details, write Penguin Group (USA) Inc. Special Markets,
375 Hudson Street, New York, NY 10014.

Jeremy P. Tarcher/Putnam
a member of
Penguin Group (USA) Inc.
375 Hudson Street
New York, NY 10014
www.penguin.com

Library of Congress Cataloging-in-Publication Data

New thought : a practical spirituality / edited by
Mary Manin Morrissey.
p. cm.
Includes bibliographical references.
ISBN 1-58542-142-1
1. New Thought.   I. Morrissey, Mary Manin.
BF639.N39   2002   2001054200
289.9'8—dc21

Printed in the United States of America
1   3   5   7   9   10   8   6   4   2

Book design by Debbie Glasserman

*This book is lovingly dedicated to the mystical Presence
that gives rise to all the world's religions and finds
its flowering in the teachings of New Thought.
This wisdom, practically applied, brings forth life,
and life abundantly.*

Acknowledgments

I wish to acknowledge the deep commitment to this project, the just plain hard work of my fellow leaders of the Association for Global New Thought: Dr. Michael Beckwith, Rev. Howard Caesar, Rev. Carol Carnes, Rev. Argentina Glasgow, Barbara Marx Hubbard, Rev. Mary Omwake, Rev. Wendy Craig-Purcell, Rev. Richard Rogers, and Dr. Roger Teel, as well as our dynamic executive director, Barbara Fields Bernstein.

A deep appreciation to Joel Fotinos for your contribution to our world and for believing in this project, and a heartfelt gratitude to Brenda Rosen for your editorial work on the manuscripts. I also thank Rachel Duvack and Chris Adams for your awesome administrative assistance. I especially want to thank my husband, Ed Morrissey, for your vision and drive for this project and for your support of this message.

Most important, this book would not exist without the efforts of our many contributors. I am so grateful for your willingness to put your words on paper so that this transforming, life-giving New Thought message can touch countless lives.

Contents

Introduction: New Living Begins with New Thinking

Rev. Mary Manin Morrissey

*As a man thinketh so is he, and as a man
chooseth so is he and so is his nature.*

RALPH WALDO EMERSON

I had ruined my life, and now I was paying the price. At eighteen, I yearned for nothing more than the simple rites accorded all my friends by virtue of their coming-of-age: fussing over a prom dress, borrowing Dad's car on Saturday nights, giddily anticipating life in a college dorm. But the life I had once assumed awaited me could never happen. Instead, I lay in a hospital bed, waiting to die.

The diagnosis was nephritis, which had destroyed my right kidney and was rapidly attacking my left. The doctor planned to remove the worse kidney and told me that if he could reduce the blood toxin level in the still functioning one, then possibly, I might have another six months.

Only six months to live? I was eighteen years old. I should have raged at the injustice but lacked the passion to object. I passed time at the hospital tucked in a blanket of self-loathing, watching soap operas and avoiding my family. Nothing had turned out the way I'd expected. And now it was too late.

Then I had a visitor, courtesy of my mother-in-law. Dr. Mila Warn introduced herself as a New Thought minister and offered to sit with me the night before my surgery. At that time, New Thought meant nothing to me. I did not have room in my mind for new thoughts, when the old ones took up so much space and repeated themselves so insistently: "You're worthless. You're hopeless. You could have done something wonderful with your life, but you've destroyed everything. What a disappointment you've been to your parents, to everyone."

I was a homecoming princess and honor student in 1960s middle-class suburbia who disgraced herself by becoming pregnant at the end of her junior year in high school. The wedding was conducted hastily at the courthouse. I wore a dress that tugged around my middle. My mother's crying all but drowned out the "I do's." When I tried to return to school the following fall, the principal sent me away to a "special" school for delinquent boys and pregnant girls in a rundown part of town. When my son was born—the first of four children—I loved him dearly, but the emotion that gripped my heart and guided my life was shame.

So New Thought meant nothing to me, but a fresh face provided a much-needed break from episodes of the *Days of Our Lives* on television and the reruns of *Mary's Ruined Life* playing in my mind.

Dr. Warn asked if I wanted to talk, and I wound up telling her everything. When I was through, she said, "Mary, your body is replicating what's been going on inside your head."

"What do you mean?"

"I mean that you've been shaming yourself because you feel like you let everybody down. That shame is toxic to every cell in your body."

My thinking was toxic? Yes, I knew that embarrassment turned my face red, that fear made my heart race, but never before had I made the connection that toxic thinking could poison my body.

Dr. Warn told me that we are children of God and, as such, inherently creative. Our Creator bestowed that capacity in all humankind. We can no more stop creating than we can stop breathing. We create, every minute of the day, through our thoughts. The thoughts that our minds cling to long enough will materialize in our bodies, our relationships, our work.

The poisonous thoughts of shame and humiliation that I'd been feeding my mind, Dr. Warn continued, may have seeped into my body, but the magnificent thing about creativity was that, at any moment, I could change my pattern of thinking. I was free to choose again. I could believe that there was a presence and a power that were greater than the disease ravaging my body. "With God," she told me, "nothing is impossible."

Dr. Warn offered me a new thought: "Imagine that when the kidney leaves your body, the toxicity that has been poisoning your life will disappear as well. Draw that picture in your mind."

The image took some effort to construct. Until that point, it had not occurred to me that my thoughts held such power. Like most people, I'd always been happy when things went well and sad when plans or hopes went awry. I had never considered that I had the power to influence events by how I chose to think about them. "Though we can't always choose our circumstances," Dr. Warn explained, "we can always create a new way to look at them."

That night, we did what she called a "sweeping prayer." We swept through my heart and mind and gathered up every bit of shame, guilt, and disgust we could find and put it into the kidney scheduled to be removed the next morning.

The surgery went well. In fact, the doctor was frankly perplexed. While my right kidney was indeed destroyed and had to be removed, the left one, which should have been only half-functioning, looked perfectly normal. "Time will tell," he said. And time certainly has. I have never had a recurrence of kidney disease.

I had thought my life was over that summer of 1967, but in truth, it was just beginning. Somebody walked through the door and gave me the gift of fresh perspective. I came to see that even the most dire situation could become a stepping stone to greater good. Sure, I had made a mistake—the biggest of my life. I had hurt my parents, forced my boyfriend to drop out of college to marry me, and created the circumstances that resulted in my life-threatening illness. Yet without my mistake, I would never have discovered my power to cocreate with God. I would never have discovered a love so deep it would change my life. I might never have become a teacher, counselor, and minister. This tremendous shame, this seemingly unforgivable act, paved the path for a greater life than I could have ever imagined. New Thought theology taught me that our mistakes are called by our souls into experience so that we can learn a lesson designed to bring us to a point of awakening.

You may not be in a hospital bed when you pick up this book, but toxic or self-defeating thoughts may be holding you back from fulfilling what you are meant to become. You may have given up on your dreams. Or, like most of us, you may have touched only a glimmer of the promise that Jesus invited us to experience when He said, "I have come that they might have life and that they might have it more abundantly."

The church I serve and founded, Living Enrichment Center in Wilsonville, Oregon, is one of nearly 2,600 New Thought congregations around the globe. One of the things that has endeared me and so many others to New Thought is that you don't have to have been schooled in or to practice a particular ideology to allow New Thought to transform your life. New Thought churches embrace all forms of loving God. New Thought is inclusive, rather than exclusive. Aristotle once said, "Those who say there is only one road to Rome don't know Rome very well." New Thought teaches us not only to tolerate but to honor all paths to God. How could a God who shows up in so many diverse ways create only one path? All religions have love at their core: We are meant to learn to love one another, to love God, and to love ourselves.

New Thought tells us that God is everywhere. There is no place that God is not. There is One Presence, One Power, One Life in all the universe. Many of us were raised to believe in two powers, one for good and one for evil. New Thought teaches that there is but One Power, just as there is a single force called electricity. It's how you use the power that makes the difference. Electricity can electrocute or it can light up a room. Just so, we can always use God's power to enlighten, to bring about good. New Thought is all about making the commitment to bringing forth the good and the beautiful in life.

New Thought had its genesis in the perennial wisdom that weaves itself through the great teachings of all times: that we are children of a wise, powerful, and loving God meant to seek and express the divine in ourselves. We believe that there is no separation between God and ourselves. Just as an elephant swings its trunk to clear the path before it, when we align ourselves with the power of God, obstacles and difficult circumstances that would have left us entangled are swept away. Our will, matched with God's, produces an energy that guides us safely forward. Thus New Thought is not just theology but a practice meant to be applied in our lives.

Moreover, New Thought is not New Age. It is not a dogmatic system of thought, philosophy, or religion. It *is* the belief that health, happiness, and success are the birthright of every child of God. New Thought "practices in the twenty-first century what Jesus taught in the first."[1] Jesus really meant it when He said, "Follow Me." We see Jesus not as the Great Exception, but as the Great Example of a fully awake being who practiced turning possibilities into reality. We, too, can bring miracles into the world. We are meant, with God's help, to heal body and spirit. We are to demonstrate love such that others are healed and made new. As Jesus said: "He who believes in Me, the works that I do, he will do also, and greater works than these" (John 15:9).

New Thought officially came into being in the mid-nineteenth century. It was founded by Phineas Parkhurst Quimby, a New England healer who believed that our faith is what makes us whole. His philosophy has been explored and expanded upon by some of the greatest minds of his and subsequent generations. Writers Ralph Waldo Emerson and Henry David Thoreau; Charles and Myrtle Fillmore, who started the Unity Movement; Ernest Holmes, who founded Religious Science; and others developed a wide range of theological and practical approaches to God with the common theme that we can better our lives by altering our thoughts.

New Thought is a collection of writings by ministers and teachers on five aspects of life molded and connected by New Thought ideals: health, prosperity, creative endeavors, relationship, and spirituality. The topic areas demonstrate that every aspect of life, from our marriages and friendships, to our physical and psychological health, to how we think about our money, can be affected positively by the power of new thinking.

[1] INTA *Bulletin,* December 15, 1916.

You might find this notion strange at first and wonder, for instance, "What does my spirituality have to do with prosperity?" Yet New Thought teaches that whatever we give—love, talent, time, or dollars—multiplies and circulates back to us. When you infuse your life and the lives around you with giving, you widen the circle of greater good. Conversely, if you don't have God, no matter how much money you have, it's never enough. Without a higher presence in your life, you will never feel secure and will always long for more of whatever you feel yourself to be lacking, whether it's love, health, or stock options. But develop a personal relationship with God, and you'll find a connection so much more compelling than any material object. As the people you are about to meet have discovered, the need to cling to your "share" falls away as the desire to share expands.

The stories contained within these pages are more practical than theoretical. They tell of people who have used new thinking to bring about healing, tap into their creativity, and deepen their relationships. They demonstrate that ordinary people can create extraordinary lives when God becomes a living reality, a comforting companion and ever-present force that leads you to develop to your highest potential. You can turn to these stories not only for inspiration but also for ideas to help guide you through a particularly dark chapter in your own life.

There is a parable about an old mule who stumbled into a farmer's well and plummeted to the bottom. He lay there, helplessly on his side. The farmer heard the mule's pitiful braying and peered into the darkness. After carefully assessing the age of the mule and the condition of the well, he decided that neither was worth saving.

"Might as well put the poor old thing out of its misery," the farmer muttered and went off to enlist his neighbors' help to shovel dirt. Their plan was to fill the well, burying the animal. When that first shovelful of dirt smacked his back, the mule panicked and brayed even louder.

Then came the next clump. As it struck, the animal pulled itself into a standing position and shook its fur free of debris. Another load fell. The mule shook it off, stepping onto the growing mound of dirt beneath him. Dust stung his eyes, but the mule kept moving. Blow after blow, chunk after chunk, the animal kept shaking off sod and dirt. The pile of dirt kept growing. The mule kept shaking if off and stepping up.

Much to the surprise of the farmer and his neighbors, it wasn't long before the old animal, battered, exhausted, and blinking away a film of dust, stepped over the wall of that well out into the sunlight.

We've all tumbled down that well into a dark place in our lives. Our bodies falter; our bank accounts run dry; the people we love most in life go away: Bad news heaps itself on us so that we can't see a way out of the rubble.

But no situation is hopeless unless we deem it so. We cannot always steer clear of life's pitfalls, but we do have the power to choose how we will respond to them. We have the power to think, to tap into universal wisdom. We can call on God. Harnessing inner resources that we didn't even know existed, we can emerge from the pit of despair stronger than ever. Like that old mule, we can *shake it off and step up*. What we thought would bury us can actually bless us.

That step out of the well into the sunlight is part of our great journey toward the discovery of our own souls. The further we venture down the spiritual path, the more aware we become that we are not traveling alone. Every time we turn to our divine companion, we are blessed with a new thought.

MARY MANIN MORRISSEY is founder and senior minister of Living Enrichment Center in Wilsonville, Oregon, serving nearly 4,000 people weekly. Mary's message is spread to more than 100 countries through radio outreach as well as a nationally broadcast television program that reaches into 18 million homes in the United States. Her latest book, *No Less Than Greatness: Finding Perfect Love in Imperfect Relationships,* teaches the spiritual principles that bring us closer to God, ourselves, and others. Her popular book *Building Your Field of Dreams* was adapted by PBS for a one-hour documentary and has been taught at churches across the country. Mary is a renowned humanitarian who has addressed the United Nations on nonviolence and has worked with the Dalai Lama. President of the Association for Global New Thought, Mary was ordained into the ministry in 1975. She also holds a teaching certificate and master's degree in counseling psychology.

Part I

Health

Introduction: The Power to Heal

Rev. Mary Omwake

The Power to heal, to prosper and to guide you,
Is not in the sky, it's deep down inside you!
J. SIG PAULSON

It's no exaggeration to say that the current revival of interest in spiritual healing began with the teachings of New Thought during the late 1800s and early 1900s. At that time, much of Christianity taught that illness was God's will and that suffering was a way to salvation. Even though Jesus declared: "It is not the will of your Father who is in Heaven, that one of these little ones should perish" (Matt. 18:14), many churches held that misfortune of any kind was sent by God and should be endured stoically. The notion that God causes or condones suffering is well illustrated by a pamphlet handed to pilgrims at Lourdes, the French shrine famous for "miraculous spontaneous healings." It reads, in part: "Most of you will return home without being cured just because it is your business to be ill. It is a most precious business, which has come to you straight from Heaven. . . . There is no other way to Heaven except suffering."

When seen in the light of New Testament accounts of Jesus' life, this attitude seems peculiarly paradoxical. Though fully a third of the Gospels focus on Jesus' healing ministry, by the late nineteenth century, spiritual healing had virtually disappeared from much of Christianity. Matthew tells us, for example, that "Jesus went all about Galilee . . . healing all manner of disease" and reports that Jesus declared, "All that I do you can do too . . . and even more can you do." Although Jesus reminded his followers that "All things are possible, only believe" and that "the Kingdom of God is at hand and the Kingdom of God is within you," these promises of a healthful and abundant life were no longer considered to be a practical reality available to all.

Recognizing that Jesus was the Great Example, not the Great Exception, New Thought took Jesus at his word and began to explore and practice the universal spiritual principles that he embodied. New Thought understands that Jesus' declaration in Luke 13 that "it is the Father's good pleasure to give you the Kingdom" refers not to a location somewhere in space or in a future time, but rather makes clear that the Kingdom of Heaven is a state of consciousness of your oneness with infinite goodness itself and is always, already at hand.

Obviously, the spiritual principles that underlie health and wholeness are not exclusive to Christianity. To further energize the revival of spiritual healing, New Thought reached out to the ancient wisdom inherent in other great world spiritual traditions. For instance, New Thought teaches that each of us is a spiritual being, living in a spiritual universe that operates under spiritual principles. It holds that we are so much more than the bodies through which our spirits express during our journey on earth. The ancient Hindu scripture the Bhagavad Gita sets forth this belief in words of timeless beauty: "These bodies are perishable, but the dwellers of these bodies are eternal, indestructible, and impenetrable." Thus New Thought set about to teach and to demonstrate what has always been true about the human condition. The essence of its practice of spiritual healing is the belief, echoed by sacred texts from every great spiritual path, that healing is possible because human life is, at its core, eternal and whole.

The New Thought approach to spiritual healing is comforting and immediate. According to New Thought, right where you are, in whatever the circumstances you find yourself, infinite goodness, as ever-present life, is expressing through you. There is no condition or challenge you face that is greater than the power of God in you. All you need to experience radiant health is to believe it is possible. You are invited to make the discovery that Jesus made, "God and I are one," and to live attuned to the flow of life. With God, you come to understand that all things are possible!

Unfortunately, most of us have come to believe that we are primarily physical beings who need something outside ourselves to make us whole or complete. Unity Movement founder Charles Fillmore challenged this mistaken notion when he wrote: "Health, real health, is from within and does not have to be manufactured in the without. It is the normal condition of man, a condition true to the reality of being." Unity minister and author Eric Butterworth concurs: "There is a divinity in man which is the whole and perfect activity of God. God's will is a ceaseless longing of the Creator working to perfect Himself in that which he has created."

Following upon these principles, New Thought teaches that you can improve the quality of your life by developing a healing consciousness. In order to reap the full promise of the spiritual principles that assure good health, you must make the conscious effort to embody these principles. Here, for instance, are some things you can do right now to improve your health and experience greater wholeness:

First, you can believe that healing and radiant health are possible. Faith is the great affirmative power that says "yes" to the infinite goodness of life regardless of appearances. We all have within us the potential for mountain-moving faith, but we must take the steps necessary to activate it.

I witnessed for myself the power of such faith several years ago, when a member of my congregation, a twelve-year-old girl named Deirdre, left for school one morning seemingly in perfect health. By six o'clock that evening, she lay in a coma as a result of Reye's syndrome. As her temperature soared to 106 degrees, the medical staff at the hospital where she had been taken used all available technology to save her life. For some period of time, the life support system that kept her breathing registered no blood flow to her brain. The doctors feared that if she lived she would suffer severe brain damage.

When Deirdre's father was told that his daughter's prognosis was death or severe mental impairment, he demonstrated some of the most powerful faith I have ever seen. He declared that his daughter was whole, and he refused to believe in any lesser outcome. He would honor her soul's choice if it was her time to make her transition, but if she chose to stay, he would not accept anything less than perfect health. He stayed in prayer for several days with people of many spiritual traditions, and everyone agreed to believe in Deirdre's full recovery. Despite several seizures and a request from the medical staff to remove the life support system so that Deirdre might pass peacefully, the father's faith never wavered. "She was whole and perfect when she left for school, and she will be whole and perfect when she returns" was his continuous affirmation. And, indeed, when Deirdre regained consciousness several days later, she was amazingly healthy except for a droopy left eyelid, a condition that quickly responded to physical therapy. My own faith increased that day, and I firmly believe that no matter what the "experts" say, no healing is impossible.

Unfortunately, I've noticed that many people fail to activate their faith until they face a crisis. New Thought teaches that faith must come first, as Myrtle Fillmore wrote: "In the silence, we shall experience the very presence of God and we shall discern just how we are to go about living this gift of life we have been given." In other words, rather than seeking God only in emergency situations, go first to God, the source of all wisdom, and then do as God directs. A regular practice of prayer and meditation helps you to be receptive to the harmonious and peaceful healing currents of life. Seeking God in the silence ensures the peace of mind that proceeds any outer manifestations of healing. "Be still and know," the ancients admonished. "God and you are one."

A second aspect of a healing consciousness is the willingness to release all unforgiving thoughts. Forgiveness is a gift you give yourself. It frees you to live in the present moment unburdened by long-harbored resentments that can block your awareness of love's presence. Not to forgive, as Gary Zukav writes, is like wearing a pair of dark-colored glasses that distort everything you look at.

Third, you can accelerate the powerful work of Spirit within you by joyously giving thanks. Your developing faith says "yes, all things are possible," and your gratitude reflects this faith in the unfailing life of

Spirit. By praising and giving thanks, you liberate the finer essence of soul and keep open the channels through which God's ever-present goodness flows.

Finally, an essential step in all healing is the cultivation of love in every aspect of your life. Love by its very nature harmonizes, blesses, and unifies. A loving attitude harmonizes mind and body and makes the maintenance of good health a way of life.

Several years ago I read the story of a young schoolteacher who was stricken with a severe case of multiple sclerosis. The disease progressed rapidly, leaving her bedridden and unable to do even the simplest tasks. Unable to work, the woman found herself consumed more and more by resentment and self-pity. Under her minister's guidance, she struggled to forgive, wrote daily gratitude lists, and tried to love her life though it had been turned upside down. As her faith deepened, there was some marginal improvement and occasional freedom from pain, but still the illness remained.

Then, on one visit, her minister suggested that she pray for others. The woman's initial response was anger. She couldn't walk or dress or feed herself, and she was being asked to pray for others? Yet, she agreed to try. She prayed first for people she knew. Then friends began to give her prayer requests. Before long she was spending almost every waking hour in prayer, even scanning the newspaper for inspiration as to where to focus her prayers. Less than six months after beginning to pray for others, she was walking again, and within a year, she was back at work, her MS in remission. This woman's story illustrates the spiritual principle that all that you give, you give to yourself.

Life is an amazing gift, to be lived, enjoyed, and shared. As the essays in this section illustrate, New Thought invites you into a continuous celebration and exploration of the healing power that is within you.

MARY OMWAKE was ordained a Unity minister in 1989. She served as an associate minister at Church of Today in Warren, Michigan, and for ten years, as senior minister of Unity Church of Overland Park, Kansas. She is a founding member of the Association for Global New Thought. In March 2000, Mary was inducted into the Board of Preachers at the Martin Luther King, Jr. Chapel at Morehouse College in Atlanta, Georgia. She speaks nationally at ministers' conferences, Youth of Unity rallies, and adult retreats and is a featured author in the books *Out of the Blue: Delight Comes into Our Lives*, *Chocolate for a Woman's Soul*, and *Chocolate for a Mother's Heart*.

The Long and Short of It

Lorra Wiggins

I remember sitting in amazement every time I'd watch our daughter Jennae' ice-skate. I expect that's true of most parents watching their children excel at something. But in our family, it was more than just being good at what she was doing. It was a constant reminder that we all have obstacles to overcome. How we choose to handle those obstacles, I guess you could say, is the long and short of it.

Jennae' began ice-skating at six. With eight competitions under her belt, yielding seven first places and one second, you'd never know she was skating with one leg two inches shorter than the other.

Jennae's obstacles began at birth. Diagnosed with fibular hemimelia, the shortening of the tibia and fibula, she taught us all a lesson in faith. When Jennae' was born, she was missing a metatarsal in her right foot. Since her pinky toe had no bone in the foot to connect to, it attached itself to its neighboring toe. In addition, the tibia, fibula, and femur of her right leg were shorter than those in her left. Because this condition causes each leg to grow at a different rate, the one-inch discrepancy at birth became a two-inch difference at six, and was projected to be three to four inches when she was fully grown.

Eight days after her birth, experts in the field of orthopedics suggested that we have her short right leg amputated at the knee. Without being able to predict how the leg would grow, doctors believed this to be the best decision. Six other specialists confirmed this diagnosis.

We've come to know firsthand that faith isn't really faith until it's all you're holding on to. With tremendous support from family, we made the decision to search for a doctor who would find a different avenue.

Had this been a life-or-death situation, we could have justified the removal of Jennae's leg. We weren't talking life or death, so I needed to find a way to stand secure in the belief that we were making the right decision. After much emotional turmoil, the answer came: "It's not my leg. I don't have the right to remove it. A decision like that can never be undone." So we moved forward in faith that a better answer was out there.

Three weeks later we found a doctor through Children's Hospital who agreed to work with what we had. His parting words have stayed with me ever since: "I will dance with your daughter on her wedding day, on her own two feet, if I'm invited." That was the attitude we were searching for.

Jennae's first year of life was spent in a series of casts designed to hold her foot in a neutral position. A one-inch lift on her shoe helped her learn to walk by the time she was one. We were now on our own, with two options ahead of us at a later date: lengthening the short leg or stunting the growth in the other.

By the time Jennae' was two, we made the decision to forego the shoe lift. This choice came easily considering that she never kept shoes on. No sooner would we get them on, but she'd take them off, as if to say, "I'm fine just the way I am." That's been her underlying attitude ever since.

Jennae' learned to compensate for the difference in the length of her legs by walking on the balls of her toes, or by tilting her pelvis so both feet could remain flat on the ground. But her own corrective measures only worked for so long. As her legs continued to grow, it became increasingly difficult for her to compensate. Jennae' decided it was time for the next step.

Barely six-and-a-half, Jennae' underwent five hours of leg-lengthening surgery at Children's Hospital. She came home two days later with two large pins in the bones of her right leg, eight surgical wires running through the right foot and shin, eight pounds of hardware to support the pins and wires, an Achilles tendon that had been cut in three places, and a bottle of Tylenol. The apparatus, called the Illizorov frame, remained attached to her body for ten months. Constant adjustment lengthened the leg a millimeter each day. Each of the eighteen pin sites had to be sterilized daily. Confined to a wheelchair for a month, then on crutches, with no ice-skating for a year or more, it's easy to see how much courage and faith she had.

As soon as she was home from the hospital, Jennae' began physical therapy sessions twice a week at the hospital and four times a day at home. Each session was painful, forcing the muscles to stretch in order to keep up with the lengthening bones.

You may wonder where the healing power of prayer or God fits into this. It's easy to say "right from the beginning," and although that's true, it wasn't always obvious back then. You see, during the ten months Jennae' wore the Illizorov frame, many complications occurred.

First, Jennae' slipped on a bead her brother had dropped accidentally. The fall broke her right femur. Now she had a body cast attached to her frame for six weeks as the femur healed. This injury interrupted physical therapy, bringing additional challenges as her unstretched muscles began to tighten. The muscles were so tight that her shinbones slipped away from the knee. The Illizorov frame had to be extended above the knee, which necessitated another surgery and more pins and wires through the thigh!

After the lengthening was finished and the Illizorov frame came off, Jennae' needed to wear a protective cast for eight weeks. Out of the cast only a month, she and her younger brother Jeremy were playing tag. They collided. The impact broke her tibia and fibula where the new bone was forming. Jennae' found herself facing yet another surgery, this time to pin the bones in place as they healed.

From the first, the goal was to lengthen Jennae's right leg enough so that she wouldn't need another surgery later on. This meant lengthening the leg eight and a half centimeters, which we did. But each setback cost us something. Breaking the femur delayed physical therapy. Without physical therapy, the muscles tightened. Extending the Illizorov frame above the knee again prevented therapy, such that she could not fully straighten her leg. Breaking her tibia and fibula resulted in the loss of new bone.

In other words, anything and everything that might go wrong did! Why? Where was God in all of this? Where was the good? Imagine a six-year-old asking why God was allowing this to happen. If God answers prayers, why not hers? Jennae' knew of others who, through prayer, had been healed. Why not her?

Yet another surgery was needed to straighten her leg. The surgery could be done now or at the next lengthening, which we all hoped would never come. Every cell in my body shouted, "Do it now. Do it now." So, in December 1999, Jennae' again had surgery. When it was over, Jennae's right leg was straight and the same length as the left for the first time in her life! But remember: we had hoped her right leg would be longer than the left because it was growing more slowly. We were still hoping to avoid another lengthening later on.

I found that it wasn't just Jennae's faith that was being tested. I found myself feeling very protective any time someone suggested that Jennae' might heal her leg herself through prayer. After a while and after so many setbacks, I found myself preparing Jennae' for the worst while only hoping for the best. This compromise became the nature of my thoughts for quite some time.

Then, in September 2000, something changed. I awoke one morning with a deep-rooted conviction in the pit of my stomach that I had never experienced. "Jennae' isn't going to need any more surgeries. Never!" But how could this be? How could I be so sure?

I found myself at a crossroads. Should I share this revelation with anyone? Should I tell Jennae', my husband, or my family about this knowing? Since there was no way I could explain my feeling, I decided to keep it to myself, in case I was wrong. "It's safer that way," I told myself. So that's what I did.

Now God has fabulous timing and a way of getting through to those who keep tuning him out. You see, the day I awoke with this certain conviction wasn't just any Monday. It was the day of Jennae's semiannual appointment, when X rays would be taken to determine the rate of bone growth. My feeling gnawed at me as we made our way to the clinic.

On the way, Jennae' (almost ten now) asked, "Mommy, do you think there's a chance I might not need another surgery?"

Still confused by my own feelings, I replied, "Let's wait and see what happens at this appointment."

X rays were taken, and her doctor, after charting the results, said, "Looks like Jennae's right leg is a half-millimeter shorter than her left." Instantly I knew something had shifted. I asked the doctor to pull the records from her last appointment. Jennae's right leg had been almost two millimeters shorter in March. Could her right leg be catching up? Could it be growing faster than normal?

The doctor's reply was definite: "No. This birth defect doesn't change. The only way the right leg would grow faster is if it had a serious injury, like a bad break. With the increased blood flow, you might see it grow a little faster, but that's not the norm."

Nonetheless, the doctor agreed that something was peculiar and suggested that perhaps she had done the math wrong at the last appointment. She decided to start with the half-millimeter difference and to wait and see what happened next.

I wish I had a tape of our conversation on the way home. Jennae' asked, "Mommy, why do you think my leg is growing faster now?"

Totally perplexed by my own feelings and the X-ray results, I turned the question back to her. "What do you think?"

"Either the doctor doesn't do math very well, or God is making my leg grow faster," Jennae' replied. "I think it's probably God."

LORRA WIGGINS has been the executive director of Church of Today in San Diego, California, for the past eleven years. She is the home-schooling mother of two children.

The Art of Spiritual Mind Treatment

Rev. James L. Lockard

When you listen to an accomplished musician, a *virtuoso,* the notes seem to blend into a single, seamless whole. A piano student at a recital may have mastered the science of playing. He may strike the keys in the proper sequence and with proper technique, but often the playing seems mechanical. The virtuoso, however, can transport you beyond an awareness of notes and technique to an altered state of consciousness.

It's also possible to be a virtuoso in Spiritual Mind Treatment or any type of affirmative prayer. When you pray with expertise, you compose and place into the Creative Medium of Mind a complete idea with images, emotion, and a perfect expectation or faith. Such prayer is creative thought of the highest order and must manifest in your life.

Spiritual Mind Treatment arises from a consciousness of oneness with Spirit, of the presence of the Christ consciousness within, of your own divine nature in full contact with infinite substance. Such thought creates a perfect sense of expectation—full faith that your word is in perfect harmony with the use of spiritual power.

The accounts of Jesus contain a number of remarkable demonstrations of this harmony, including several healings. In each case, Jesus is perfectly calm, perfectly at ease. He engages in no ritual, no chanting, no extraordinary actions of any kind. When healing is requested, he asks, "Do you believe that you can be healed?" If the answer is yes, he makes a definite statement, such as, "Arise and walk; your faith has healed you." Then he goes on about his business.

What was Jesus trying to teach by these actions?

Mary Baker Eddy said that Jesus was the most scientific man who ever lived. She meant that he understood and used spiritual laws by directing his creative thought from a position of full expectancy or perfect faith. Whether the outcome was restoring a sick person to health or multiplying food to feed the many, the use of the law was identical. Jesus taught, "Pray believing you have received, and you shall receive."

That simple statement is the key to Spiritual Mind Treatment. Only believe that you have received, that your desire is already here, fully accomplished, right now, and it must become so. Not in the future, not contingent on any outer person or circumstance, not at the whim of some moody god. Your desire is fully present in potential right now and always. Manifestation comes when you fully accept this fact at a level of knowing.

Knowing is more than believing. You can believe something that you do not know. You only know that which you have experienced. You believe many things that have never happened and are not likely to happen. Belief alone does not cause manifestation. Ernest Holmes said that what you do not personally experience is just theory. The theory may well be true, but you only know that which you have experienced. So Jesus taught you to know that you can manifest healing, abundance, and love. But how do you know to a sufficient degree to manifest these effects when you have not had the experience? How do you move beyond theory in Spiritual Mind Treatment?

Let's go back to our virtuoso pianist. How did he get to be a virtuoso? We can be certain that he first learned the mechanics—the science—of playing music and the theory of proper technique. Then he practiced—and practiced and practiced and practiced. He practiced until his playing seemed effortless. As he practiced and continued to learn new things, the pianist built up a consciousness of competence and a consciousness of positive expectancy. He mastered the intricacies of playing the notes and reading the music; he mastered the skill of learning new material and playing in various circumstances.

Then, perhaps, one day, he reached a point in his regimen of practice and learning when, for just a moment, in one piece of music, he transcended the mechanics. He moved beyond the notes, the technique, the music, and just played. He knew immediately that something had happened, both within and without. Within, he felt a difference; the music came from a higher place—from somewhere seemingly beyond him. Without, the music changed, perhaps only in a subtle way. But for that moment, he played at a higher, transcendent level. Then, the moment passed.

The pianist was amazed and fascinated. He played the piece again, but the moment did not reoccur. The pianist was at a point of choice. In that instant, he could decide that the experience was a fluke, not likely to be repeated, or he could begin with determination to redouble his efforts to re-create that moment of transcendence.

Since the pianist in question became a virtuoso, he must have made the latter choice. He must have practiced and then practiced some more until that moment came back again and again. He practiced until that moment came to dominate his musical life, until he could decide very calmly to put himself there at will.

Jesus must have done the same thing. But as is the case with the virtuoso, we rarely see the practice, the preparation. It appears that spiritual talent springs onto the scene fully developed. But, no. It is not like that.

The art of Spiritual Mind Treatment is mastering the mechanics through practice, practice, practice—writing, reciting, rewriting; constantly directing your thought toward your desires, toward the idea of a loving Spirit of which you are a blessed part. When your thoughts stray, you return them to that central idea, daily, hourly, moment by moment.

The art of Spiritual Mind Treatment is the art of seeing only perfection, only that which is desired—seeing beyond conditions or appearances to the greater spiritual truth. When Jesus came upon the blind man, he did not see a blind man. He saw the perfect potential of vision behind the condition of blindness, and he made a definite statement corresponding to spiritual law to allow that perfect potential to manifest. Jesus supplied the consciousness of ability to see the perfect spiritual potential so clearly and to know that the law must operate so as to manifest such a knowing. The blind man provided a consciousness of receptivity to healing, regardless of who or what he believed was the healing element. The joining of perfect knowing with perfect receptivity created the necessary conditions for manifestation to take place.

If you are practicing Spiritual Mind Treatment for yourself, receptivity must be a part of the knowing in your own consciousness. You do not need the experience of a certain thing or condition to manifest it, but you do need some experience of the creative process. As you engage in Spiritual Mind Treatment, you gain the experience of the creative process at work, and manifestation starts to happen at a certain level. Later, you use the same process in a new circumstance. As you repeat this process over time, your sense of knowing grows.

Just as Jesus knew that his word would be accepted by the Creative Medium of Spirit, you can know that your word will be accepted. The Creative Medium is not more receptive to one person's knowledge of spiritual law than to another's. It is accepting of all requests that come at the level of knowing, rather than at the level of belief. Whatever you know about yourself right now is manifesting perfectly in your life.

As Ernest Holmes wrote in *The Science of Mind*: "To think of Jesus as being different from other men is to misunderstand his mission and purpose in life. He was a way-shower and proved his way to be a correct one! His method was direct, dynamic, and powerful, yet extremely easy and simple to comprehend. He believed in God in himself, as Power and Reality. Believing in God within, he was compelled to believe in himself."[1]

The art of Spiritual Mind Treatment is mastered by awareness plus practice. Through awareness, you incorporate the words, images, and feelings of what you desire into a single thought entity—a single state-

---

[1] Ernest Holmes, *The Science of Mind* (New York: Dodd Mead and Company, 1938), 367.

ment from a consciousness of perfect expectancy, planted as a seed of intelligence in the fertile soil of mind. When such perfect thoughts are nurtured, they are acted upon by the creative principle and come into manifestation in your experience. Constant practice helps you reach a level of transcendent awareness and knowing so that the use of these principles comes to dominate your life.

When you become a Spiritual Mind Treatment virtuoso, you consciously choose the circumstances of your life. Of course, you may have already chosen them, perhaps at an unconscious level. There is no transfer of power. The power is in Spirit, but it must be directed by your individual consciousness. When you realize this fact fully—really know it—using your thought as a power for healing or for any other positive manifestation becomes as direct as flipping the light switch and expecting the lamp to light.

You are a potential prayer virtuoso. You can make the choice to bring the abundant gifts of spiritual law into your life for healing and for any good purpose. The notes of your life can blend into a seamless whole of awareness and transcendence.

JAMES L. LOCKARD was the founding pastor of Religious Science Baltimore, one of the fastest-growing New Thought churches in North America. Since January 2000, he has been pastor, with Dr. Arleen Bump, of the Ft. Lauderdale, Florida, Science of Mind Center. Before beginning his ministry, he worked in law enforcement in Maryland and Florida. He is the author of *Survival Thinking: For Police and Corrections Officers* and is a frequent speaker at both law-enforcement and New Thought conferences.

Getting to the Truth of the Matter

Rev. Bill Worth

The neurologist gave me one of those looks. You know, the kind you never want to see from a neurologist who has been reading an MRI scan of your brain.

"I'm sorry to have to tell you this, Mr. Worth, but it's pretty clear that you have multiple sclerosis."

It was 1989. For weeks, I had been besieged by violent headaches, so painful they incapacitated me. My wife, Nancy, and I were preparing to leave our home in Maui because she had been accepted to ministerial school at Unity School for Religious Studies at Unity Village, Missouri.

Starting this training fulfilled a long-held dream for Nancy, and while I had little interest in living on the mainland again, I had agreed to accompany her. From Maui to Missouri—what a letdown! Yet I feared that our relationship, which had been strained in recent years, required my presence during her two years of study for the ministry.

But now those headaches! They began at the back of my head, on the left side. Within minutes, it felt as if my brain were a nail, and the world was a hammer. My HMO doctor had referred me to a neurologist, who examined me carefully and paid close attention to my most recent medical history. One clue he seized on was that shortly after moving to Maui from Ohio in early 1983, I had lost the vision in my left eye for a week or so. Gradually my vision returned, but the optic nerve had been damaged, and the sight in that eye had never returned to normal.

The neurologist had sent me to Honolulu for an MRI. Now I was back in his office, feeling very alone, as the neurologist explained that the test showed that I had been stricken by a progressively debilitating disease.

"There is no cure for MS," he told me. "It will get worse as time goes by. Eventually, it will cripple you, and you'll have to live in a wheelchair. And sooner or later you'll die, probably from complications caused by the disease."

The disease affects the myelin, he explained, the sheath that surrounds nerves. When the myelin weakens, the nerves "short out." Thus one symptom of the progress of the disease would be numbness in my extremities. He showed me the MRI scan, pointing out the bright parts that showed MS lesions on my brain.

Though I was trying to listen, I could hardly focus on what he was saying, until he added the only note of hope in the entire conversation: "Usually, this disease hits younger people. Maybe you've had it for twenty or thirty years, and it's just showing up now. That may indicate that yours is a mild case that will take a long time to get really bad." I was forty-seven years old. It was cold comfort to think that I'd be living with a disease that would take a long time to get "really bad."

Yet, at that moment, a powerful idea entered my mind, which I immediately translated for the neurologist: "Doctor, you say I have multiple sclerosis, and you may be right. But I say, multiple sclerosis does not have me!"

Time went by. After a short course of steroids, my headaches gradually diminished. We moved to Missouri. I took a year off to write a novel, and then worked part time for *The Kansas City Star* as a copy editor during Nancy's final year of schooling. My health was fine. I had no further symptoms of MS. Nancy graduated and accepted a ministry in Tallahassee, Florida. I got a job working for the Florida Department of Natural Resources in its public information office.

In 1992, my feet went numb. I visited a physician, who listened carefully to my medical history, put me through another MRI, read the results, and agreed that I had MS. He prescribed steroids, which I took. The numbness went away.

In 1994, I applied to ministerial school at Unity Village and was accepted. Part of the curriculum required students to examine their "core issues." Self-reflection helped me to realize that my most serious core issue was an ongoing problem with relationships. Further self-examination revealed some interesting connections between this issue and my health challenge.

I learned, for instance, that *sclerosis* means "hardening." So, I had a disease that manifested in my body as "multiple hardenings." Through meditation, I came to see that, for many years, I had hardened myself to life. I had chosen a profession, newspaper work, that valued a stance that was aloof, removed, objective, and not involved. In other words, my life's work rewarded me for being "hardened" to human emotions, the sorrows and joys evoked by events in the news everyday.

I had learned to repress my emotional nature: first, because I am a male; second, because I was a journalist. When I was brought up, in the late forties and early fifties, it was made clear to me that "big boys don't cry" and that boys were considered "sissies" if they displayed real emotions. Journalism simply reinforced that belief. To do a good job, a journalist had to be removed from the story. Becoming involved or feeling the events too keenly meant that a reporter could not describe events clearly and objectively.

So here I was, learning to be a minister, afflicted with "multiple hardening" of my emotional nature—so much so that it was playing out in my body as an incurable disease.

I decided to look into my heart for the answer. I changed my approach to life. I decided to be open, rather than closed. I decided to risk being hurt in relationships rather than trying to stay uncommitted. I decided to feel.

It was a real stretch, and some days, it still is. Sometimes I still close myself off and have to remind myself that I do not want another "hardening" to add to those that caused my disease.

It's been almost eleven years since the neurologist gave me that look. I experience some numbness in my extremities now and then and an occasional "flare" of muscle pain and fatigue. However, I am not confined to a wheelchair. I am not an invalid. I work fifty or so hours a week and even get out on the golf course fairly regularly. I know I am not cured of multiple sclerosis, but I am convinced I am healed.

You see, I know the truth about me. I am not a victim. I have multiple sclerosis, but it does not have me. And most important, I have learned a valuable lesson: When you want to get to the truth of the matter, you have to go first to its heart.

BILL WORTH is co-minister, with his wife Rev. Nancy Worth, of Unity Church in Christ in Tallahassee, Florida. Before entering ministerial school, he spent thirty years as a newspaper journalist, serving as reporter and editor for daily newspapers in Dayton, Ohio, and as editor and publisher for the weekly newspaper in Lahaina, Maui, Hawaii. He has written articles for *Unity Magazine* and is a published poet and the author of a novel.

Realizing Oneness . . . Upside Down

Rev. Nancy Worth

I was driving down a little back road near Unity Village one day in the spring of 1991. I was a month away from graduating from ministerial school. It was a dreary day with a light rain, and the roads were a little slippery. My husband, Bill, was following me in our other car because we were heading to an appointment, after which he had to go on to work, and I wanted to go home.

I skidded a little around one curve, so I slowed down, but then I came to a sharper curve and hit an especially slick spot in the road. I started skidding and sliding. Not knowing what to do, or what not to do, I hit the brake, which was not a good thing because that started me spinning. Before I knew it, my car hit the edge of the road on the opposite side. The wheels on one side of my car began to lift off the ground, and the car rolled down the embankment into a cow pasture below.

I thought, "This is it!" and my life began to scroll before my eyes like a motion picture. For a brief moment I realized this really could be it, but then, as the wheels lifted off the ground, I had an incredible inner knowing that, whatever happened, I would be OK. I understood clearly, for perhaps the first time in my life, that I was connected to something much greater than my own little, limited, fearful mind.

I not only felt, but I knew, God was with me, taking care of me, guiding me, protecting me, loving me; whatever happened, I knew it would be OK. What followed was a sense of peace like I've never felt before. I was enveloped in a ball of light, and in every cell of my being, I knew all was well.

The next thing I remembered is hanging upside down. I looked around and realized I was still on this planet. The car had come to rest, and I calmly undid my seat belt, fell to the roof of the car, which was now beneath me, turned off the engine, and climbed out of the back of the car with Bill's assistance.

A coworker from Silent Unity drove by, realized it was me, stopped, and I knew that as soon as they heard what had happened, Silent Unity would begin prayer. When the officers and paramedics arrived on the scene, they were amazed that I was walking around, calm and in one piece. One officer said, "You are a miracle!" to which I answered, "Yes, I am!"

Since that experience, I've come to realize that the time we spend on this planet is an opportunity to begin to understand our relationship with God and, in the process of that relationship, to be transformed. After rolling my car over and walking away without so much as a scratch, a bump, or a bruise, how could I not believe that I was connected to something infinite and very powerful, a presence that is incredibly loving?

Our relationship with our Creator is one of the most important, the most intimate, the most loving relationships we will ever have. We have been given this gift of life, and we are the ones who choose how to use it. Recognizing this gift starts with each one of us inviting the presence of God into every area of our life—not just on Sunday at a church service or in prayer and meditation—but into every relationship, every circumstance, and every experience.

What we experience comes, at some level, out of some thought we hold in mind. Our thoughts can be conscious or unconscious, inherited from others or unique to ourselves. Our thoughts take form according to our beliefs. As Jesus put it, "According to your faith let it be done to you" (Matt. 9:29).

In every moment of our lives, we are creating, either consciously or unconsciously, experiences we are happy about and experiences we wish were different. We have the power within us to determine what shows up in our lives and how it shows up.

Even the feeling of being discontented or unsettled is a divine gift. If you've been discontented or unsettled or had a feeling there's something more, that's a divine gift. That's how our lives get our attention and begin to speak to us. The yearnings and desires of our souls are God speaking to us, calling us to a higher level of being. Life is saying, "There's more. Don't settle!"

In *The Power of Myth,* Joseph Campbell wrote: "People say that what we're all seeking is a meaning for life. I don't think that's what we're really seeking. I think that what we're seeking is an experience of being alive."

When we experience our connection to God we find that our capacity for living life to the fullest increases. Right here in this moment, we couldn't be any closer to God. Yet, we keep searching. Carl Jung had a sign above the door to his home that read, "Called or not, God is present."

Let us remember that we are created in the image and likeness of our Creator, which is whole and perfect and pure. God already knows this; now it's time for us to believe this about ourselves.

For a long time I never realized what the problem was. I thought it was other people, where I was, what was happening, my job, my health, my relationships. Then I discovered what "it" was; "it" was me! When we make that connection to the One Presence and One Power that is God, it's astonishing the things that can happen in and through our lives.

Maybe we don't have to roll cars over to realize our oneness. Or maybe we do. Whatever your dramatic encounter with Spirit is, open your heart, listen, and then follow where it directs you to go or what it tells you to do or be.

The day I rolled my car over, I knew I was connected to something infinite. I realized oneness . . . upside down. Sometimes our lives have to be turned upside down to know that God is protecting us and guiding us, all the time.

NANCY WORTH is the founding minister of Unity Church in Christ in Tallahassee, Florida, where she serves as co-minister with her husband, Rev. Bill Worth. Before entering the ministry, she was a professional dancer on and off-Broadway and on national and international tours. She has worked as a telephone prayer worker for Silent Unity and as a counselor at the Unity Village Counseling Center and is trained as a hospital and hospice chaplain. She has written a column titled "Community of Faith" for the *Tallahassee Democrat* as well as articles for *Unity Magazine*.

That Darned Drawer

Rev. Pat Palmer

That darned drawer kept sticking! One of the advantages of having my own office was being able to work right along, in my own fast-paced style. It always caught me by surprise when that sticking drawer on the left side of my desk interrupted my flow.

Maybe this particular day that sticking drawer seemed even more disruptive because I was so happy. The Center for Conscious Living, the first group I had founded as a Religious Science minister, was two years old and growing steadily and healthily, or at least it seemed so to me. We had relocated to a beautifully appointed office building. My office space was particularly breathtaking. One wall was glass, and from my desk I looked out over a lake, manicured lawns, and Florida palms and willows. As my eyes took in the peace during telephone calls and counseling sessions, I very often gave thanks. Being at my desk heightened my awareness of existing simultaneously on the material and the spiritual planes.

This particular day, I was in the midst of putting together an event for the center, doing several things at once, when that darned drawer stuck again! This time I did not take the time to get down in front of it, like I usually did, hitting it gently and evenly on both sides to nudge it back into its track so I could close it. (Don't even ask why I had never had the drawer fixed. That answer would probably be a good example for Stephen R. Covey's *Seven Habits of Highly Effective People,* in the "important but not urgent" category that suggests less effective functioning!)

I was on a roll, doing things pretty unconsciously, and I didn't want to let a stuck drawer slow me down. Ever force anything? Well, that's what I did. I hit the drawer hard with the heel of my left hand, and it closed all right. The only problem was that I had neglected to clear my fingers from its path. The middle finger of my left hand was hanging over the front edge of the drawer, giving me a good grip on it. As it slammed shut, my finger was mashed.

I do not think I remember ever experiencing such pain! It was so intense that I did not even cry out. I was in shock, I guess. The pain filled me. I moved as though in a dream. Without conscious intention, I slowly raised my left arm in the air and spread my fingers. I remember swiveling my chair so that I was looking out the window next to me, and I held my hand toward the sky. I closed my eyes, I think, and directed my total attention to the throbbing. I became that strong pulsation and felt myself move into the intense pain. My mind had merged with the tip of my finger. There was no separation.

At that instant, the pain vanished completely. I gradually lowered my hand, staring at it in disbelief, and then I slowly began to smile, looking out to the nature I loved, and saying "Thank you, thank you."

And that was the end of it. No bruise, no losing my nail, no reminder except in my heart. It was one small event, in one typical day, but it changed my life forever. I experienced the power of letting go, of being with whatever is happening without resistance. I was led into living what I teach, and I knew I had been blessed.

PAT PALMER is founder and pastor of the Center for Conscious Living in Clearwater, Florida. He holds degrees in mathematics and counseling. He makes frequent presentations for organizations on the subject of quantum physics and metaphysics.

Churches as Healing Communities

Robert Ellsworth, Ph.D.

I t amazes me to realize that faith communities have existed and thrived for centuries in every part of the world. As early as 50 B.C., the well-traveled Greek philosopher Plutarch observed: "If we traverse the world, it is possible to find cities without walls, schools or theaters, but a city without a temple or one that does not practice worship, prayers and the like, no one has ever seen." Even in parts of the world unknown to Plutarch, native peoples gathered to worship, celebrate, and relate to the divine.

Plutarch's observation is as true today as it was over two thousand years ago. Could it be that churches, temples, and other places of worship came into existence because they meet essential needs in ways possible by no other organization or group? Throughout the New Testament, we read that many who came to "house churches" experienced emotional and physical healing. They also came to hear the "Word," spiritual teachings that changed their lives. They prayed together and supported one another in fellowship.

Is the same true today? A leading health researcher, physician Jeffrey

Levin, has found conclusive evidence that people involved in faith communities, whether they be Christian, Jewish, Muslim, Hindu, or indigenous peoples, are physically and emotionally healthier than those not so involved. After reviewing over 250 studies, Levin concluded: "On this point there can be no argument. A positive association between religion and health has been observed in hundreds of studies of various designs, conducted by scores of researchers in different countries."[1] Levin further pointed out that scientists have largely ignored these findings because of their personal bias against religion.

What accounts for these remarkable findings? Levin identified three components found in faith communities with links to physical and emotional healing:

1. *Positive belief systems.* Research indicates that positive beliefs enhance optimism and self-esteem, strengthen the immune system, hasten recovery from illness and depression, and promote longevity.

2. *Connecting and belonging.* Studies show clearly that people in relationships live longer, recover from serious heart attacks more quickly and completely, and resist viral infection better than those who remain isolated.

3. *Prayer.* Several researchers have concluded that people who pray experience various kinds of emotional and physical healing.

In our book, *Vital Signs of a Healthy Church,*[2] my wife Janet and I identified four additional components with links to physical and emotional wellness:

4. *Uplifting, sacred worship.* Worship services that are both uplifting and practical make a positive difference in people's lives.

5. *Empowerment.* A safe, encouraging faith community empowers people to take life-changing steps.

---

[1] Levin, Jeffrey S. "Religion and Health. Is There an Association, Is It Valid, and Is It Causal?" *Soc. Sci. Med.* 38, no. 1 (1994): 1475–1482.
[2] Ellsworth, Robert B., and Janet B. Ellsworth. *Vital Signs of a Healthy Church: Seven Keys That Heal, Empower, and Grow Congregations,* Pathfinders Ministry. P.O. Box 2302. Lee's Summit, MO 64063.

6. *Meaningful small groups.* Prayer circles, study groups, and other communal meetings deepen people's sense of belonging. As people share their deepest feelings and concerns, they often enhance healing on physical and emotional levels.

7. *Positive serving experiences.* Surprisingly, studies show that people who regularly volunteer need less surgery and suffer fewer serious illnesses. Most people who serve others also feel an increase in energy and optimism.

Since we wanted to help leaders assess and meet their congregants' vital needs, we constructed and field tested a sixty-item church life survey.[3] Results from more than seven thousand surveys collected in more than fifty churches show that both congregants and leaders play a role in creating communities that positively impact people's lives.

We found, for instance, that congregations in which a high percentage of people say that "belonging to this church makes a positive difference in my life" are alike in a number of significant ways. In greater than average numbers, people in these churches report that they learn and practice "positive beliefs," "connect" with other church members through classes or other small groups so that they feel a sense of "belonging," practice balanced "prayer," and feel themselves to be part of a community environment that "empowers" them to make positive life changes.

It comes as no surprise that these seven factors also help churches themselves stay healthy and growing. Our research found that ministers and leaders of thriving churches create "uplifting sacred worship services" by giving inspiring and practical sermons that send listeners away feeling not only uplifted by a sense of God's presence and love, but with an experience of emotional release as well.

Moreover, church leaders in healthy churches provide classes and other ways for people to learn and practice "positive beliefs," "empower" members by helping them identify and use their spiritual gifts, and provide "meaningful small groups" in which people feel heard

[3]Ellsworth, Robert B., and Janet B. Ellsworth. "Church Life Survey." Pathfinders Ministry. P.O. Box 2302. Lee's Summit, MO 64063.

and have the opportunity to share prayer requests and outcomes. Churches who score above the norm in these areas thrive because their members often invite others to join and because these newcomers often stay and become part of the faith community.

The word "church" comes from a root that means "to swell; to be stronger; to be a hero." It seems clear that faith communities have survived and thrived over the years because they have helped their members swell, or grow, in physical, emotional, and spiritual strength. Churches have heroically taken on the task of meeting vital needs that impact the well-being of the people who belong to them. The seven elements of church life described here not only further the spiritual growth of healthy congregants but they encourage churches to grow and thrive as well.

ROBERT ELLSWORTH is co-minister, with his wife Rev. Janet Ellsworth, of Pathfinders Ministry in Lee's Summit, Missouri. Formerly director of education for Unity Churches, he has also worked as a research clinical psychologist. For three years, he and his wife traveled to churches throughout the United States presenting workshops for both ministry team members and congregants. He is author of three books published through Thriving Churches Ministry: *Building an Effective Prayer Ministry, Come Apart for Awhile: Exploring Four Ways to Pray Taught by Jesus*, and *Vital Signs of a Healthy Church*. He can be reached through his website, www.thrivingchurches.org.

The Healing Balm of Spirit

Sage Bennet, Ph.D.

When I first became acquainted with New Thought teachings about twenty years ago, I was attracted to two points. First, I agreed with the emphasis on demonstrating spiritual principles in our everyday lives. Second, I believed in the power of mind and Spirit to heal conditions.

Nothing is as convincing as our own experience of healing. When I found myself with a serious gall bladder condition, I remembered the healing potential of New Thought philosophy. The healing words of New Thought writers, such as Ernest Holmes, Emma Curtis Hopkins, Mary Baker Eddy, and Thomas Troward, were like seeds ready to fall on the fertile ground of my receptive consciousness:

> Now the principle universally laid down by all mental healers, in whatever various terms they may explain it, is that the basis of all healing is a change of belief.
>
> THOMAS TROWARD[1]

[1] Thomas Troward, *The Edinburgh Lectures on Mental Science* (New York: G. P. Putnam), 74.

The perception of wholeness is the consciousness of healing.

ERNEST HOLMES[2]

Yet you must be sure that whatever health is brought to mankind, it all comes from God.

EMMA CURTIS HOPKINS[3]

Here is my story of healing.

Almost two decades ago, I found myself in what mystical literature calls "the dark night of the soul." My marriage had broken up. My thirteen-year-old stepdaughter was undecided about where she wanted to live. I was returning to my university position in Wisconsin after an eight-week grant in California, which meant that I had to find a new place to live before fall classes started. I had recently recovered from double pneumonia. Now I was having gall bladder attacks that immobilized me and forced me to rely on prescription pain medicine.

Midday one Friday, I met with my HMO physician in a small white room to discuss my latest test results. After scanning the sonogram scans, he began to write his chart notes. "You're in danger. I need to schedule you for surgery Monday morning to remove your gall bladder."

Lying uncomfortably in a scant, paper dressing gown, I looked up from the metal examination table unable to fathom how I could handle surgery and six weeks of recovery with everything else I was facing. "What are the alternatives?" I asked the doctor, who continued to write.

"There are none," he answered.

Ironically, his words gave me hope. I had a background in philosophy, and one thing I knew was that there are always alternatives. I had also been reading *Spirits in Rebellion,* the classic text on New Thought. I remembered being inspired by testimonies of how mind and Spirit were agents of healing. Here was a chance to participate in my own healing.

I got off the table, still in pain, yet hopeful about healing. During

---

[2] Ernest Holmes, *The Seminar Lectures* (Los Angeles: Science of Mind Communications), 15.
[3] Emma Curtis Hopkins, *Scientific Christian Mental Practice* (Marina Del Rey, CA: De Vorss and Co.), 145.

the next few days, I vacillated between the relief of not being cut open and the fear engendered by my doctor's warning, "You could die, you know." Still there was something within me that knew that healing was possible.

My life reflected the insight of St. John of the Cross. The dark night of the soul is a time when our familiar structures of life crumble—in my case, marriage, family, and familiar surroundings. After the death of the old structures in the dark night experience, we have to rely more and more on God, our true foundation. I had to rely on God because that was all I had left.

My inner, intuitive voice began to soothe me with assurance. "You are guided by the wisdom within. Repeat to yourself: 'The love of God surrounds me. I walk in the peace of God.'"

In Wisconsin in the early 1980s, holistic health was not as widely known as it is today, but I had heard of a chiropractor who was attuned to spiritual healing. After calling several doctors who refused to treat me because of my serious condition, I called him, the last number on my list. It was after five o'clock on a Friday afternoon. To my surprise, Dr. Bircher answered the phone. I explained my condition. "Can you help me?" I asked, clearing my throat.

The voice on the other end was clear and simple. "Sure," he said.

I felt my body relax. My pain diminished. I was witnessing how the conviction in the possibility of healing is healing itself.

Over the next weeks, I devoted myself to mental, spiritual, and physical healing. I repeated to myself many passages from *The Science of Mind*. I especially liked this one:

> By some inner mystic Presence,
> I was told to live and to love, to laugh and be glad.
> I was told to be still and know of the One Almighty Power,
>   in and through all.
> I was told to let that Power work through and in me.
> I believed that voice and I received my Good.
> I am healed—the Joy of Life . . .[4]

---

[4] Ernest Holmes, *The Science of Mind* (New York: Dodd Mead and Company, 1938), 521.

I rested, fasted or ate light meals, and continued to work with my holistic chiropractor. Loving friends came to visit and pray with me. I played the piano. I forgave my ex-husband and released resentments of the past that until then I didn't even know I had.

Yet I think the most important thing I did was to create a place for the healing balm of Spirit to permeate my life. I immersed myself in the healing presence of God as I meditated in candlelight. I would sit regularly in a comfortable, brown-tweed recliner, watching the flame that lit the darkness. In the stillness, bathed in the radiance of Spirit, I felt deep peace.

In six weeks, I felt much better. I returned to the medical community for another sonogram. The gallstones were gone. The technician said there must have been a mistake with the first scan. My university colleagues said eliminating gallstones was impossible. I knew I had experienced a healing.

Traditions of wisdom in New Thought—through the writings of Ernest Holmes, Phineas Quimby, Thomas Troward, Emma Curtis Hopkins, Charles Fillmore, and others—invite us to heal our lives. No matter what the condition—relationships, money, or physical or emotional disturbances—we can surrender to the wholeness of God that is in, around, and through all things and is available to us all in each moment.

SAGE BENNET is an assistant minister at the Agape International Center of Truth in Culver City, California. She is also dean and serves on the faculty of the ministerial graduate school Holmes Institute, Los Angeles. She has taught philosophy, world religions, and women's studies at the University of Kentucky, the University of California, and the University of Wisconsin, as well as at other spiritual and business centers. She has hosted a weekly radio interview program and has written for *Science of Mind Magazine*, and she is a frequent presenter and workshop leader at national conferences.

Alive, Alert, Awake, and Enthusiastic about Life

Rev. Diane Scribner Clevenger

You've all had the experience of coming into a shopping center and trying to locate yourself. You find one of those maps that has an arrow and a little sign that says, "You are here." I like those, because you've got to know where you are in order to orient yourself to your world. "You are here." Have you accepted that? You may as well face it. This is it—as good as it gets. It is not a rehearsal. This is life.

And so, the question becomes, "How am I going to show up? What am I going to do now?" I'd like to suggest an affirmation that really captures the best you can be: *I am alive, I am alert, I am awake, and I am enthusiastic about life.* That statement is the ideal of practical Christianity. It is, in fact, what Jesus meant when he said, "The Kingdom is at hand." The Kingdom is right now; that's the whole teaching. This life is your holy temple. Accept it. Live in it. When you think of that map of life, I invite you to see an arrow right above your head that says, "You are here." This is the place where you're called to witness the Kingdom.

It's fine to have goals and destinations, but the real question is, are you going to enjoy the journey? Our society is very goal oriented. We make to-do lists and chart out the future on our calendars. Our culture says that you have to know what you're doing, even two or three months in advance. All that planning for the future makes it tough to be right here, to remember that this is it—your life. So, what's it going to be?

During funerals, most clergy say at some point in the service: "Ashes to ashes and dust to dust." Those words leave you with a kind of musty, dead feeling in your mouth, don't they? But there is another line that must be added: "To the eternal soul in you that is alive, alert, awake, and enthusiastic, God bless you on your way. Congratulations! You made it. Your soul got so big, your body couldn't house it anymore. Thank you, God."

Because, after all, we are so much more than dust. Truly, we're heaven sent. I propose that we are vibrating, never-ending energy—much more akin to stardust than to the ashes and dust of this earth. Master teachers know that. Moses knew that we were stardust. Buddha, Mohammed, Nelson Mandela, Martin Luther King, Jr., physicist Stephen Hawking—they have all been aware that we are so much more than we appear to be. When we are living alive, alert, awake, and enthusiastic lives, when we're really firing on every cylinder, we express the Christ essence, which is ever renewing.

So, you might accept that you are alive. You're not ashes and dust just yet. But then the question becomes, are you alert? Are you paying attention? Are you responsive to your environment? When you're truly conscious of where you are—listening, watching, waiting, seeing truly what you have—the world flashes into meaning. Take coincidences, for example. Two things happen at the exactly the same moment for divine purpose. They are co-incidents, and they point out something great to you—perhaps some piece of the divine plan. When you are alert to coincidences, life becomes very interesting. Watch for coincidences, because they're signs that Spirit is calling you to pay attention every step of the way.

The next word in the affirmation is "awake." Though you might think you are awake right now, remember what the Buddha said when somebody asked him, "What are you?" He replied, "I am awake." So, being awake means a lot more than not sleeping. The early Christians knew about the real meaning of being awake. In Paul's letter to the Church in Ephesians, he said, "Awake you who sleep. Arise from the dead and Christ will give you light." Paul wasn't talking to prone bodies. He was talking to beating hearts, thinking minds, and searching souls. In Aramaic, the language Jesus was said to have spoken, the word *sleep* means the same thing as "drunkenness." So, essentially, what Paul was saying is, stop drugging yourself with habitual ways that lull you into doing things just because you've always done them. Stop being drugged by that fear, abuse, or anger that keeps you drunk in your response to this world. Awake from the "not enough" that you do with unproductive thinking. Arise from that dead old way. When you really wake up, you allow divine intelligence to come forth, and divine intelligence is that energy of God that moves you forward.

When you're awake, it's easy to be enthusiastic about life. Enthusiasm is actually a form of exercise. When you are enthused in some way, actual physical changes take place in the body. Structures in the brain release endorphins, the thyroid releases hormones, and you become, literally, enthused metabolically. Your blood flows better, your respiration and heart rate speed up, pain is eliminated, your mood elevates, and you experience a feeling of well-being. When all these endorphins are flowing, life gets really juicy! You are, as the word *enthusiasm* itself tells us, "inspired, possessed by God." You are lit up like trees in autumn, glowing with yellows, oranges, and reds. You see that you, and everything in this world, is on fire with the energy that gives all things life—on fire, in fact, with God!

Those of you who are runners know exactly what I'm talking about. They call this feeling "a runner's high." I can testify to it; I am a running addict, and that juicy, full of life feeling is one of the reasons I run. I want to give my body every ounce of energy that I can possibly pull up into the present moment, because, frankly, sometimes I am so low in my emotions that I need it. Now here's the great news: You don't have to be a runner to send those happy endorphins racing through your body. Laughter brings them on as well, as does a feeling of joy. Love does the same thing—reaching out, hugging someone, helping someone, taking a moment apart to sense the life force that's in all things. These enthusiasms are, in effect, inner exercise—jogging on the inside—because they cause endorphins to be given off. Laughter and love can literally make you high on life. I encourage you to try more of that!

The Lord of your being has given you this life to be your holy temple. "You are here." This is the place to recommit. You have been up and you have been down. You have been in and you have been out. You may have had to recommit to your life many times over the years. But right now, in this present moment, is the time to feel that regeneration, to affirm—in fact, to shout out loud—that you are alive, alert, awake, and absolutely enthusiastic about the wonderful gift of life you have been given! So be it.

DIANE SCRIBNER CLEVENGER is senior minister of Unity of Roanoke Valley, Virginia. She has served as the vice president of the Association of Unity Churches, Eastern region, and on the board of directors of Big Brothers and Big Sisters. She served as the PBS host of Blue Ridge Public Television's production of Mary Manin Morrissey's *Building Your Field of Dreams* and has created a CD of music and meditation titled "Pray Attention . . . With Yourself." She has participated in Unity mission work in Costa Rica and Honduras and is a frequent facilitator and presenter at New Thought seminars, retreats, and workshops.

Part II

Prosperity

Introduction: The Door of Possibility

Rev. Howard Caesar

Abundance and prosperity do not come to you, but through you. Because thought is creative, your consciousness helps to create your life experiences. Whether your river of good flows richly, trickles, or dries up depends as much on your beliefs, opinions, and attitudes as on external circumstances. Thus you can open the door of possibility to abundance or obstruct it from within.

The same principles of creation apply to prosperity as to painting a picture. Every creation starts with a passionate desire and the decision to seek an end result. If your passion is for painting, you do all that you can to ready yourself. You gather a canvas, brushes, an easel, and paints. You formulate an idea of what you want to create. If passion is present, inspiration and the ways and means to carry it out follow. What's essential is that you're one with the project, immersing yourself in it in a healthy way, confident that it can be accomplished, and filled with the love and joy of entering into a creative venture.

A similar process fuels the creation of prosperity. Ideas are the currency of the universe. You prepare yourself for prosperity by gathering healthy, expansive, creative ideas and then entering into relationship with the field of all possibilities. The more you immerse yourself in the belief that prosperity is possible, the more confidently you activate the laws and principles of abundance.

The most prominent of these is the law of cause and effect. This idea can be stated in many ways: "As in mind, so in manifestation," or "What you think about expands." Many principles are offshoots of this law, such as "Give and it shall be given to you," "As you sow, so shall you reap," and "Forgive and ye shall be forgiven." These principles demonstrate that we each must take responsibility for the conditions of abundance that we experience. As we activate from within the infinite intelligence of God as the One True Source and begin to function more completely in alignment with God's nature, our needs will be met—and beyond.

Divine principles, such as the law of cause and effect, operate the way they do because everything in the universe is energy. When the appropriate spiritual principles are applied and practiced, in effect, we position ourselves internally as an open vessel through which the abundant creative and manifesting energies of the divine can flow. God can only do for us what He can do through us. We actualize our capacity for abundance by learning to channel this flow in constructive and productive ways.

All of us have known people from humble backgrounds, of limited education, or with certain odds against them who have become successful and even wealthy. Their river of good flowed abundantly because they were willing to enter into a creative relationship with the universe. Their success involved decisions, choices, faith, optimism, guidance, actions, and a way of thinking that caused doors to open and opportunities to manifest. Though the events of their lives seemingly happened to them, on unseen levels, they helped to make their lives happen.

The laws of abundance dictate that everyone involved in a creative project share belief in its fruition. If several people are involved in the pursuit of a goal, and each holds in mind the idea of success in a pure and powerful way that exudes integrity and wholeness, there is literally nothing that cannot be accomplished. Mountains will move, circumstances will shift, and God will take pleasure in giving every participant a piece of the Kingdom they have helped to frame.

Finally, divine principles teach us that we increase our capacity for abundance by recognizing that prosperity includes more than money and material possessions. It includes health, happiness, friendships, satisfying employment, the right place to live, peace of mind, and the expansion of all that could be characterized as God's good. In other words, even if our economic status is meager, we can be rich in blessings. As Jesus said, "I come that they may have life and have it abundantly." By this he meant that we should not settle for a limited understanding of a rich and full human life, for "with God, all things are possible."

When a vision becomes clear and the possibility of its reality is nourished over time, amazing things result. I have seen this miracle happen over and over in my own life, as well as in the lives of countless others. Those who have experienced a "spiritually based manifestation" know what I am talking about and do not question the validity of this phenomenon. In the section that follows, you will read many stories that illustrate how lives are changed when the door of possibility is held open.

Let me tell you a story from my own life that illustrates this principle. My wife and I were raised in Wisconsin. We both grew up in houses that sat on at least an acre of land. We were used to the open space and liked not feeling fenced in. Our first ministry was in the state of Washington. Over time, we were able to have a home with a sizeable yard and a view of Mt. Rainier and the Olympic Mountains. We loved the wide open feel and the beautiful view.

When I accepted a new ministry in Houston, it was a big adjustment. The homes we could afford were close together, and the yards were small and closed in by wooden fences. The house we bought was fine in itself, but I felt hemmed in. We moved in, but we never gave up searching for a home we could afford that had a larger yard, or backed to a greenbelt, or had more of the feeling of openness we had come to love.

One day, we went to the office of a builder who had in his office a scale model of a development that showed the streets and the size of the lots. Each lot was marked with a red tack that meant it was sold or a green tack that meant it was available. My eyes were drawn immediately to the largest lot in the development. Its lengthy back property line was right on a golf course. "That's the lot I want," I said to the salesman.

"I'm sorry. It's taken," he replied. He tried to offer other lots, but none met our criteria as this one did.

My wife and I went out to look at the lot and fell in love with it. It was elevated above the golf course, overlooking three side-by-side fairways woven around a small lake. It had the expansive feeling and the beautiful view we were looking for, and we could afford it.

We looked at the builder's model homes and found one in particular that we felt was perfect for our family's needs. We learned that this model was designated to be built on the lot to which we were so drawn. We also learned that there were some legal matters having to do with property lines that needed to be resolved before construction could begin on the lot.

For some unexplainable reason I had been drawn to that piece of property, and although it had been sold, something kept me from releasing it and looking for something else. Something inside me told me that circumstances could change and that somehow things would work out. My wife and I told the builder that if, for any reason, that lot became available, he should call us. We continued to visit the empty lot weekly to walk around on it and imagine how nice it would be to live there. I even used large rocks, pieces of wood, empty cola cans, or whatever I could find to mark the corners of the house and garage so that we could visualize how it would be—the size of the yard, the landscaping, the patio, and possibly, a pool.

We did all this despite the fact that the model in the builder's office still showed a red tack on "our" lot. Yet, we listened to our inner guidance and never felt that we were out of the running or that something couldn't happen to pave the way for us to live there. Somehow, we believed that God had guided us to this piece of land and that the door of opportunity had not yet closed. Over the months, as we periodically stopped by to visit the property, we even got to know the neighbors in adjacent homes.

Then, one day, one of these neighbors stopped my wife in the grocery store to tell her that the lot was being turned back to the builder because the owner was tired of waiting for the legal matters to be resolved. Needless to say, we were elated! Two days later, we put money down on the house we had always envisioned for our family. After another year, the property line issue was resolved, and construction began. Though the cost of the home had increased due to the long wait, the builder honored the original price, and we moved in with even more equity than we had imagined.

Our experience taught us never to close the door of possibility on a dream. Patience and perseverance can pay off. We felt all along that God was in no way steering us in a different direction. So, we held fast to our faith that as cocreators with God, another dream would be realized.

We have been in our home for ten years now, and what makes it so special is that we are convinced that God intended it to work out this way. With God, the door of possibility to abundance is never closed.

HOWARD CAESAR is senior minister of Unity Church of Christianity in Houston, Texas, which was voted "Best Place to Worship in Houston" by *The Houston Press Magazine* and by a city-wide reader poll in *Inside Houston*. His inspirational "Thought for the Day" messages are broadcast twice weekly on radio, and his Sunday lessons are broadcast on cable television. He is the recipient of the 1997 Voice of Unity Award for excellence in radio and television broadcasting outreach. A member of the leadership council of the Association for Global New Thought, he has also served on the board for the Association of Unity Churches.

Is There a Balloon in Your Basket?

Rev. J. Douglas Bottorff

Years ago, I attended a New Thought church service as a guest. A man came in and sat next to a woman he apparently knew. They were seated directly behind me, so it was easy to overhear their conversation. In a cheerful voice, the man asked the woman, "How have you been doing?"

Equally cheerful, she responded, "Fantastic! How about you?"

"Great," he said. There was a moment of silence; then the man leaned in close to the woman and, in low tones, asked, "How are you *really* doing?"

This time the woman's response was not so positive. Before long, they were engaged in an exchange of detailed descriptions of a long list of woes.

This experience illustrates a mistake that I have seen people of faith frequently make. They confuse the pretense of happiness with actual happiness, believing that if they *act* positive, put on a bright, cheerful smile and convince everyone that they don't have a care in the world, they will somehow make a breakthrough in spiritual awareness and achieve the high-quality life they crave.

It's the old "fake it until you make it" attitude. This trick may actually help people break the pattern that ties them to addictions or other undesirable behaviors. But in the arena of spiritual development, faking it produces only a face that looks happy. Behind the smile is usually a heart that is laboring under a heavy weight of despair.

Imagine that you have a bushel basket. In this basket you place a large balloon filled with air. You then fill the basket with apples, covering the balloon. To all the world it appears that your basket is full of apples. But you know that buried beneath the apples is a large, empty space. Suppose you were to sell your apples, not by the bushel, but by the pound. Perhaps you could fool the world into believing that your basket was full, but could you fool the scales?

The scales of divine justice are much more exacting. At some point we must come to realize that our quality of experience can never outweigh the quality of our consciousness. Pretending, regardless of how we rationalize it, does not make it so. Spiritual growth is not about *rationalization;* it is about *actualization.* It's not about building high-maintenance facades; it's about experiencing genuine happiness—filling to overflowing the empty space we feel inside. Operating from the experience of this inner fullness, we bring our external life under the prospering influence of our conscious connection with God. The result is a prosperous life.

If we try to reverse this order—use spiritual means to produce material wealth so we can *then* be happy—our quest for inner peace and satisfaction will remain an unquenchable longing. We will always be a few apples short, so to speak, of a full life. We cannot experience the satisfaction we so deeply crave until we establish a meaningful relationship with that cosmic activity that bubbles like a hot spring of inspiration at the core of our being. Observing the activity of God within so that we understand what it is and how it works is the highest, most stabilizing, and most prospering act in which we can engage. Dissatisfaction results from a merely conceptual relationship with God. We will not know true and lasting fulfillment until we resonate in unity with the creative intentions of that divine force that rises up to indi-viduate itself as us.

Over the years I have come to embrace three basic truths as the guiding principles in my life. I'd like to share them here.

1. *I lack nothing.*

Many make the mistake of interpreting the emptiness they feel as generated by some incompleteness, either in themselves as individuals or in their lives. In a universe consisting only of omnipresent good, neither can possibly be true. Nothing needs to be added to you or to your life for you to begin solving your life's problems permanently. You do not need a healthier body. You do not need a better job. You do not need a life companion. You do not need to further your edu-cation. You do not need a better understanding of metaphysical prin-ciples. These will, if necessary, come in time.

Now, at this moment, you are in possession of everything you need to initiate the greatest transformation in yourself and in your life that you can possibly imagine. All that you must do is turn the power of your attention away from your endless grasping for things outside yourself and direct it to that inner spring of Spirit that flickers at the core of your being. Do this, and everything else will fall into place.

2. *I seek only God.*

All mystical traditions advocate that seekers relinquish material de-sires. Perhaps this admonition conjures up the image of an emaciated Hindu sadhu, dressed only in a loincloth, who sits all day on a rock contemplating the meaning of life. This image frightens us because we have a mortgage to pay, a family to feed, and aspirations that, more likely than not, require financing.

The mandate to release material desires, however, does not have to be the all-or-nothing proposition it may at first seem. Jesus illustrated how this can be so in the parable of the buried treasure. In the Gospel of Matthew, Jesus told the story of a man who found a treasure buried in a field. Seeing the great value of the treasure, the man sold every-thing he had so that he could buy the field (Matt. 13:44). We gather from this story that the treasure was worth more than the sum of all the man's earthly goods. Having possessed the treasure, the man would be able to buy back the equivalent of all he sold and still have abundance left over.

In spiritual terms, the buried treasure represents the expansion of consciousness that comes from experiencing unconditional communion with God. This communion allows you to reclaim your wholeness and to eliminate from your consciousness such negative influences as fear, guilt, and self-doubt. When the energy you have given to these negative states is redirected in more creative ways, you can make healthier decisions in your affairs. Once you have found such a treasure, you can evolve a truly successful life, both internally and externally.

By seeking God only, we are not donning a loincloth to please a deity who has an aversion to material wealth. We are simply complying with the natural process of prospering from the inside out. As Jesus taught, we seek first the Kingdom—being willing to sell all we have to buy the field that contains the buried treasure—confident that everything necessary for fully prosperous lives will then be ours.

3. *I will maintain my spiritual integrity.*

Self-honesty is vital to spiritual progress. We cannot afford merely to *act* happy when the alternative is actually to *be* happy. Pretending is a self-imposed obstacle to genuine happiness.

Begin where you are. Go within yourself with an attitude of humility, not as a groveling worm, but as an empty vessel ready to be filled. Be willing to lay aside all preconceptions, all knowledge you believe you have acquired about the spiritual path. Approach your inner sanctuary as a humble student who knows nothing, who is teachable, who is willing to know all. This level of integrity will carry you into a firsthand experience with God.

If there is a balloon in your basket, it is better to pop it, even if it empties half your basket. The half that remains full is genuinely yours. "For," as Jesus asks, "what does it profit a man, to gain the whole world [convince the world that your basket is full] and forfeit his life?" (Mark 8:36) What profit is there in looking the part, when you can actually have the part? Why pretend that you have a great life, when you actually have everything you need to create a great life?

Begin in the quiet, at the source of your being, and you will soon find that you will have more apples than your basket can hold!

J. DOUGLAS BOTTORFF is minister of the Mountain Light Unity Church in Evergreen, Colorado, where his congregation is currently building a new church facility. He is author of numerous multimedia projects and articles for *Unity Magazine,* as well as several books, including *A Practical Guide to Meditation and Prayer* and *A Practical Guide to Prosperous Living.* He is currently working on *A Practical Guide to Overcoming Pitfalls on the Path* and is writing a novel.

Money Is God in Action

Dr. Roger W. Teel

In no other area of daily life is there more superstition, misconception, struggle, and fear than in our relationship with money. Our culture has bestowed such mystique upon money, attributing to it power to direct our lives and bring us security, fulfillment, and even happiness. We also blame money for just about everything that can go wrong, setbacks, betrayals, divorces, compromises and poor decisions, enslavement to jobs and relationships that aren't fulfilling, and much of the world's suffering and injustice. It's amazing how we allow these bits of paper or metal to do so much, almost to run our lives. Imagine our peace of mind if we could discover a "spiritual bottom line" where money is concerned.

Western culture is generally oriented to the outer, physical side of life. Many hold the view that humans are physical organisms in a purely physical universe. However, a growing number of people have come to realize the limitations of this narrow viewpoint. They have awakened to the understanding that we are spiritual beings living in a cosmos that is essentially divine. Embracing the inner, invisible side of life and self makes it possible to awaken to the inner side of money as well. Beyond its mere physical substance and its practical uses in the world, money has a spiritual dimension. When we understand money's spiritual side, our entire relationship to it can be transformed.

New Thought teachings guide us to the awareness that each person is an aspect of the One Life, an expression of the universal source. Our central spirit is the very essence of God, uniquely expressing as who we are. All things have their surface dimensions, yet they have as well a center, a reason for being, and an essential spirit. Money has these outer and inner dimensions, too. We will never master money in our lives until we create a relationship with it based on spirit, not just on substance. A spiritual relationship with money requires that we think about its quality—what it means and what we can do with it; not just its quantity—how much we have or wish to have. The Bible encourages us to "give unto Caesar that which is Caesar's, and to give unto God that which is God's." When we discover and work with its inner, spiritual dimension, money can become a tool for awakening and empowerment.

The founders of our country must have understood something of money's inner qualities. They realized, for instance, that using money requires a basic trust not unlike our trust in God. That is why on every U.S. bill or coin are the four words "In God We Trust." The implication of this motto is that our trust in God, the One Life, should carry over to our trust in the value of money and the ways that we can use it for good.

Many other details of the design of our bills and coins underscore money's spiritual dimension. Dollar bills and coins of every denomination are inscribed with the Latin phrase *E Pluribus Unum,* meaning "the many out of the One." This phrase reminds us that behind what looks to be a multitude of things in life, there is ultimately only the One Unity, which is God. The dollar bill also contains an image of the Great Seal of the United States. It bears the mystical Latin phrase *annuit coeptis,* which means "God blesses our undertakings," a powerful affirmation that good works can be carried out through the spirit of money. The seal also contains the phrase *novus ordo seclorum,* meaning "a new order of the ages." These words speak of the new awakening to Spirit as the All. The most striking feature of the Great Seal is the image of an unfinished pyramid, a symbol of everything that we still desire to create. In the space between the pyramid and its capstone is an eye, symbolic of the all-seeing eye of God. The light rays around that capstone convey the message: "If thine eye be single, thy whole body will be filled with light." The separated capstone also reminds us that our lives and our nation are incomplete unless they are crowned with the activity and guidance of the infinite. Thinking about the rich spiritual symbols that adorn our money starts to spiritualize our relationship with it.

To deepen this spiritual outlook, we can remember that there is only One Power in this universe, One Life, and that is the Life of God, the unifying force, expressing as all things. We might think of this force as the divine energy that gives rise to all other forms of energy in the material world. It is ever seeking to create, to sustain, to guide, and to evolve. If all things emerge from this divine energy, then money, too, is divine energy at its core. It is a vehicle for the force of creativity, faith, and truth—the highest potential in every relationship given a convenient form. Seen in this light, money is a symbol of the "commerce of Spirit," the evolutionary thrust, ever seeking to build up life.

Money, then, the very energy of Spirit, is God in action. If you understand that money is essentially spiritual energy, you sense that just as there is no shortage of divine energy in the universe, there is no shortage of money. You may not always have all of the physical form of money you desire, yet since you are an expression of the divine energy, of the Holy One, then you are also one with the essence of money in its total abundance. This understanding is the first step to mastering money in your life.

Second, remember that God is love. The essence of the divine energy as it forms the universe is love. Thus, the essence of money must also be love—the love of God finding a way to build up life, to create flow and progress. Therefore, money is also love in action. Many of us were taught when we were children to fear God, who may have seemed like an angry parent who might punish us for wrongdoing. Though we might think that we have outgrown this childish belief, it is natural to project such fears onto the world around us. Many of us may have transferred our fear of God onto other obvious sources of energy in the world, such as money. We may fear that we will never have enough or that we are unworthy to have the money we need. Others may deeply resent money because they feel that someone—perhaps the fearful, parental God of childhood—has denied them access to it.

Overcoming these fears and resentments means accepting whole-heartedly that everyone and everything in the universe is part of the One, whose ultimate impulse is love. That divine energy that is God steps itself down to take the form of other energies and forces at the physical level. As is the case with any form of energy, we choose how we relate to it. We can use the energy of electricity, for example, in constructive or destructive ways. In the same way, relating to money in terms of scarcity, fear, and subconscious rejection gives money the power to destroy our peace of mind. But when we understand that money represents the love of God, money becomes a constructive force for good. We begin to release our fear and to enjoy money, no matter how much we have, because we are communing with its essence. Relating to money in this new way makes us a magnet to at-tract more of it.

Each of us is privileged to be a point of distribution for money. When we know money as love, as God in action, then we start circu-lating money with understanding and joy. Money is called currency because it is part of the divine current, the universal flow. With this awareness, we can enjoy and participate in the commerce of Spirit. As Walt Disney declared: "I've always been bored with just making money. I've wanted to do things. I've wanted to build things, get something going. I'm not like some people who worship money as something that you've got to have piled up in a big pile somewhere. I've only thought of money in one way and that is to do something with it."

So, start building your abundance consciousness by realizing the higher truth about money. Watch carefully how you talk about it and how you think about it. Whenever you notice old fears, scarcity think-ing, guilt, and the like, use them as cues to initiate higher awareness, to dispel fear and activate love. Whenever you handle money, bless its inflow and outgo. As a child of the universe, feel wealthy. Never tinge that which is love with resentment or fear. Cultivate a sharing spirit when paying bills. Receive money easily. Pause often and declare: "Money loves me and I love money. I deal honorably and powerfully with money. As a point of distribution for the love that is money, I am a powerful being. I choose to distribute it wisely, to create compassionately and purposefully with the money that flows to and from me. Money is no longer a compulsion. It is a spiritual impulsion with which I am blessing life. With joy, I open my life to money."

Money is God in action, love in action. Your relationship with money will never be the same when you really understand this. Fear falls away, your money life becomes spiritually aligned, and a healthy personal economy naturally results. Money, then, becomes your partner in creating an awakened life and a vibrant world!

ROGER W. TEEL is senior minister of the Mile Hi Church of Religious Science in Lakewood, Colorado, a spiritual community with over 10,000 members that has recently added a multipurpose facility to its futuristic sanctuary building. The Mile Hi Church's weekly television program, *New Design for Living,* aired in Denver for over nineteen years. In addition to lectures and workshops for service organizations, schools, and businesses, he is a frequent presenter at national conferences and retreats and is a founding member of the Association for Global New Thought.

I Dare to Be More Prosperous

Rev. Wendy Craig-Purcell

Try saying this sentence out loud: "I dare to be more prosperous." How many of us can say those words with conviction? What's expected of us if we accept that dare?

Many of us believe metaphysically that the universe always says "yes" to us, that "It is the Father's good pleasure to give us the Kingdom." But the abundant and prosperous life we desire will not be handed to us on a platter. First we have to seek the Kingdom; only then, as Jesus told us, "All these things will be added unto us." In other words, God does not take a step toward us until we take a step toward God. We must do our part. Doing our part requires some work, some growth, and some change. In a minute, I'm going to lay out six simple steps you can take to accept the dare to be more prosperous, but first let's consider what's at stake.

There's a wonderful story that illustrates the pitfalls of refusing to play our part in creating our own prosperity. It concerns a general contractor who had been very successful and had, as a result, become very prosperous. As he was getting ready to retire, his daughter became engaged to an up-and-coming young contractor. The father called the young man to his side and said, "You know, I've had it very tough in my life. I want to do something special for you. I want to start you out with a job where you can earn a good deal of money. Here is what I want you to do.

"I want you to build me the finest, most beautiful house you can imagine. Put in the very best of everything—the very best flooring, the very best wood, the very best tile, the very best appliances. I want it to be a premier house.

"Of course, I also want you to write a very healthy profit into it for yourself."

The young man was very excited and agreed instantly. But as soon as his future father-in-law's back was turned, he thought to himself, "This my chance to make a killing." And so, he went about drawing up plans and constructing the house using inferior products and inferior subcontractors, while building in an inflated profit for himself.

The house was finished in record-breaking time because the young contractor paid no attention to detail. When all was completed, he presented the bill and the deed to his future father-in-law.

The father-in-law glanced at the bill and immediately wrote out a check. Then he took the deed and tore it into pieces. "I've wanted to give my daughter a jump start in life," he said with a smile. "The house is yours. You built it for yourself."

Imagine the young man's astonishment and chagrin! Do you think he would have made different choices if he had known that the house was for him?

The point of this story is that you are always, always building the house for yourself. You may think that you go to work for someone else. The truth is, no matter who signs your paycheck, you don't work for somebody else; you work for yourself. The house you are building is your life. You have no choice about whether you are going to build a life or not. Since you are here living and breathing, you are building some sort of life. The choice is whether you are building that life by design with a plan in mind, or whether, like the young contractor in this story, you are building a life by default and by drifting, by cutting corners and ignoring the details. When you're not consciously and deliberately making the choices in thought, feeling, attitude, and behavior that construct a quality life, a life with substance and purpose, the only person being cheated is you.

So, what must we do to accept the dare to be more prosperous? What spiritual principles must we follow to construct an abundant and meaningful life?

There's no way around it: the first principle is giving. To dare to be prosperous, we must learn to give joyfully, with no strings attached. Though some of us have mastered giving joyfully, we give with strings attached. We want to be sure that our giving is acknowledged, that the person knows what a sacrifice we made to do whatever it is we have chosen to do. This kind of giving is actually bartering or exchange, and the universe doesn't reward that. What is rewarded is giving joyfully, without expecting anything in return; as Paul says in the New Testament, "God loves a cheerful giver."

Cheerful giving is a struggle for most of us. It's a skill that we must choose to practice consciously as part of our path toward spiritual growth. Many New Thought churches encourage their members to adopt the practice of tithing, or at least proportionate giving. Tithing comes from the Old Testament, which tells us to "give back to God ten percent of all that we receive." Proportionate giving is donating a percentage—though not necessarily ten percent—of all one receives. The truth is, of course, that ninety percent of what we have *with* God will always go further than one hundred percent *without* God, but this idea is really tough for many people to swallow. Though I don't know how to make tithing more palatable, I do know this: Those people who practice tithing or proportionate giving as an aspect of daring to be more prosperous will find that their lives work at a level that would be impossible otherwise. When we fail to give generously and cheerfully, the only people we ever shortchange are ourselves.

The second step in daring to be more prosperous is learning to become good receivers who can accept and acknowledge gratefully the good that comes into their lives. A good receiver has a heart that says, "Thank you, God, for all the good that comes into my life—the big good as well as the little good." Does it make sense that if we are unappreciative of the little good, the universe is going to reward us with great good? Why should it? The great good is going to flow to those who are appreciative of whatever good they receive.

Part of being a good receiver is being receptive to ideas that can translate into products or services that other people want. I know some people who think that all they have to do to become prosperous spiritually is to pray, affirm, visualize, tithe, and then just sit back and wait for God to come to their doors and say, "Here it is." But that isn't how the universe works. You have to keep your eyes and ears open. You have to have an idea that is worthy of people wanting it.

You might be saying to yourself, "But, I don't have any ideas." The truth is that the ideas are out there, and they're free in the sense that they're available to each of us. The price is that we have to pay attention. Perhaps there has been a time in your life when you didn't have enough money for something you really wanted to do, or enough money just to meet your needs. For some of you, this may be true right now. I know this is hard to accept, but when this situation occurs, the problem isn't money. Lack of money is the symptom. The real problem is lack of ideas. If you can focus on ideas, be open to them, believe in them, and be receptive to God's help, you will have all the money you need.

Being receptive to God's help means that you practice being aware of the divine impulses in you to do certain things or to try certain things. How do you know when what you're feeling is a divine impulse? Here are a couple of things to look for. If what you're feeling is a divine impulse, you will feel energized, enthusiastic, excited. So watch for a flow of energy that you didn't have before you caught that idea. The other sign to look for is that a divine idea is "bigger" than you are, so much so that it tugs at you to grow in at least one way. So watch for those divine impulses that give you energy and cause you to stretch.

The third step in daring to be prosperous is forgiveness. When we don't forgive, we become blocked. Think about this principle just in terms of our relationships with others. When we refuse to forgive another person, we feel blocked in that relationship. The love doesn't get out, and the love doesn't come back. The same holds true in the rest of life. When we are unforgiving, when we are closed up inside of ourselves, there is no room for God to move through us with ideas. So we must ask ourselves, "What am I still holding on to? Who or what do I need to forgive?"

Forgiveness also means learning to handle yourself graciously, without ill will toward others. I read a story sometime ago about the actor Kevin Costner. He had a very small part in the movie *The Big Chill*. When it came time to put the movie together, the director, Larry Kasdan, decided that he had to cut out Kevin Costner's part entirely. He called Costner into his office and said, "I'm really very sorry, but I've had to rework the movie and cut out your part, so you don't even show in the movie. I truly apologize."

Costner was tremendously gracious in how he handled the situation. He said, "Larry, being in this movie has been the experience of my life. It has shown me what kind of actor I want to be, and I wouldn't trade it for anything. You have nothing to apologize for. You have given me a great gift."

A friendship between Kasdan and Costner started at that moment. When Kasdan wrote the film *Silverado,* he wrote in a part for Kevin Costner, which launched Costner's career. Any ill will on Costner's part would have blocked this gift. Because he was gracious, great good came to him.

The fourth step in daring to be more prosperous is knowing what you want. Be so clear about what you want that you can write it down so that somebody else can understand it. In fact, do write it down! Be as specific about what you want as you possibly can, but then—and this is critical—leave room for God to work something even bigger if that's meant to be. Once you've written down what you want, refer to your goals frequently. When you think about them, pray about them, and visualize them, come from the place of knowing that this goal is what you're desiring but that you're also open to something better.

The fifth step is to ask God to show you what you need to change about yourself in order to create the life you want. You can't keep doing the same things that you've always done and expect different results. You just won't get them. Different results come from doing different things or doing the same things in different ways.

Here's the shortest book in the world. Chapter one says: "I walked down a path not seeing a dog. The dog bit me." Chapter two: "I walked down a path pretending not to see a dog. It bit me." Chapter three: "I walked down a path, saw a dog, but I let him bite me out of habit." Chapter four: "I walked down a path, saw a dog coming toward me, and ran away from the dog. But the dog caught me and bit me anyway." Chapter five: "I walked down a different path." The point of this book, of course, is that if you keep doing what you've always done, you will get what you have always gotten. Something in you has to change, and change consistently, in order for you to prosper.

What are the kinds of things that you may need to change? Ask yourself, how's my attitude about people and about life in general? Do I need to learn some new skills? How are my people skills? How are my work habits? I believe that how we show up in one place in our lives, say at church or at work, is how we show up everywhere else. So pay attention to what needs to change in order for you to get along better in every arena of your life and then make the necessary changes.

The last step is very simple. Take action. In Unity we use affirmations and denials a lot. These are valuable tools. But I've been in Unity more than half of my life now, and I've known too many people who use affirmations, treasure maps, and visualizations without ever taking action. A number of years ago, I coined an expression to address this problem: "It's time to get up off your affirmations and do it." Think of that great Nike commercial, "Just do it." Take a deep breath and remind yourself that there is no growth without change, and there is no change without some discomfort. Say out loud, "I dare to be more prosperous," and then just do it.

WENDY CRAIG-PURCELL is founding minister and spiritual leader of Unity Church of Today in San Diego, California. The youngest minister to be ordained in Unity, she hosts a weekly inspirational radio message and was the recipient of the 1998 Sir John Templeton Radio Grant. She is also the recipient of the 1999 Mahatma Gandhi Non-Violence Award from the Tariq Khamisa Foundation. She serves on the board of the Foundation for Affordable Housing, is chair of the Church Growth Committee of Unity, and is a member of the Leadership Council of the Association for Global New Thought.

Missing the Mark with Abundance

Kathy Gottberg

Last week I had the opportunity to sit down and talk with a new friend about spirituality. Although I enjoy all types of conversation, the truth is, I would rather talk about our interconnectedness to all life than any other topic. I warm when the talk turns to how that interconnectedness has made a difference to my life, my community, and the entire planet. Yet in that recent conversation, running underneath my favorite subject, I noticed a shadow. Rather than ignore it as we all too often do, my new friend and I included it in our discussion. Maybe it's time we all did. That shadow is the obsession with money in our society and in some of our spiritual organizations.

My background in New Thought was heavily steeped in abundance and prosperity thinking. Actually, that was one of the first attractions I had to this sort of teaching. Although I always had faith and a deep conviction in Spirit, it was a bonus, especially during the eighties, to find out that God supported me in creating riches. I attended Sunday services almost like sales rallies or weekly motivational meetings. New Thought taught me that not only did I deserve to be abundant but also that by using spiritual principles, I could actively cocreate an affluent lifestyle. Affirmative prayer and other positive-thinking practices boosted me toward my goal of success. I began to see money as spiritual energy and learned ways to attract more of it into my life.

Of course, I ended up learning a lot of other things as well. Even though the majority of my classes focused on success and prosperity, I fortunately didn't stop there. I began learning about myself; I began learning about consciousness; I began learning the true nature of God—all in spite of myself. In retrospect, one of the hooks that got me involved in New Thought may have been prosperity. But the reason I stayed, the reason I'm still there today, is for Spirit.

My New Thought path brings to mind the infamous quote by Ernest Holmes, founder of Religious Science. He said, "If you need an aspirin, take an aspirin." In the eighties, in a culture bent on having it all and making as much money as possible as the true indicator of a life well lived, many of us certainly needed that aspirin. Now, though some of us have come to realize that there is much more to life than consumerism and acquisition, too many of us still play that game, still base our lives on those outdated values. Unfortunately, so do many of our churches and spiritual organizations. Perhaps it is time we all grew up.

As my friend and I acknowledged in our frank conversation, with all the talk of trusting Spirit as the ultimate source, many a church discussion is as scarcity minded as a dinner-table talk about shrinking household finances in any home in America. When new members attend a leadership meeting at church for the first time, they are often shocked to discover the similarities. Those that have been in the fold and know the ropes pat the naive ones on the back and remind them that in order to succeed, a church must be run like a business. And recognizing business as the ultimate authority in America, the newcomers usually end up agreeing with this assessment. I know that drill, for that's exactly what I used to believe.

Call me slow, but during my recent conversation, I realized for the first time that something was really wrong with that picture. Instead of standing by and watching leaders teach people that church is just another business, shouldn't we be reminding one another that a true spiritual organization answers to a higher standard than "good business practices"? Instead of trying to convince one another that it's okay for a spiritual organization to work as hard on its bottom line as it is to work on Spirit, perhaps we should question what that organization is really teaching and promoting.

These musings bring to mind the passing of two famous women who symbolize our confusion over abundance. When asked who they would rather be, Mother Teresa or Princess Diana, most people would say that they certainly admired Mother Teresa, but they'd admit that they had a hard time seeing themselves walking through the slums of Calcutta in her shoes. Rather, the woman most of us would choose to emulate was Diana. Her beauty, intelligence, good works, and yes, her money, made her a highly envied woman on the planet, a princess whose lifestyle many of us would love to experience.

Yet, I think it is pretty obvious that of the two women, the one who was the most privileged, the most materially abundant, was the least happy. Although Mother Teresa spent every day of her life in material poverty, she spent it in love. Her life was full, complete, and "on purpose." When Westerners asked Mother Teresa if they should move to India to help her, she reportedly told them to stay in their own country and work with people there. She said, "I have never seen such loneliness as the poverty of affluence in America." Mother Teresa considered affluent Westerners to be as "poor" as the people of India. Maybe she had a point.

Now don't get me wrong. I am not advocating that we deny that money has an important place in our lives. I realize it is hard to be spiritual when you don't have money to pay the rent or take care of basic necessities. I enjoy having a nice house, a nice car, and nice things. But I also want to remember and to promote actively the truth that life is so much more than acquiring things or amusing myself. As Lily Tomlin noted, "The trouble with the rat race is that even if you win, you're still a rat." I want to remember that. I'd rather be known more for the good that I spend my money supporting and promoting than for what I've just bought. In the words of Lynne Twist, one of the founders of The Hunger Project, "I want to be remembered for what I allocate, rather than what I accumulate."

I think our spiritual organizations should represent these values as well. After all, we all say that we believe that Spirit comes first and that all else will then be added to us. Yet, too many people have confided that in some organizations, by some teachers, they have felt compelled to want more money or more things just to fit in with the crowd. It is one thing to help people rise above a sense of limitation and lack, and quite another to shame them into believing that there is something wrong with them if they aren't bitten by the abundance bug. Certainly television, the newspapers, and our workplaces have a constant campaign to sell us on the primacy of money. Shouldn't there be at least one place in our lives where we can escape from that pressure to be controlled by money and to conform?

That safe haven should be our spiritual organizations. It is time for us all to demand that all groups that represent Spirit champion our highest ideals. Obviously, the healing available through New Thought principles stands for much more than using Spirit as a big ATM machine. Yet many of us have stood quietly by and allowed our own and our society's obsession with money to seep into the very fabric of our teaching. Saying "It's All God" is not the same as saying "It's All Money." But unfortunately, in some churches, they sound too similar.

It is right that we should ask the highest of our spiritual organizations. By doing so, we expect more of ourselves. If we truly believe that we are spiritual beings first, and that consciousness precedes form, let's demand that our spiritual organizations and the people who lead them show us the way. And let's not be afraid to speak up when any of us miss the mark.

KATHY GOTTBERG is one of the founding directors of the Palm Springs Center of Positive Living, an organization dedicated to exploring and practicing New Thought principles and the new science approach to organization, leadership, and community. A frequent lecturer and workshop facilitator, she has written for *Unity Magazine*, *Science of Mind Magazine*, and *Quest Magazine*. She is currently working on a novel based on New Thought ideas.

Prosperity Consciousness

Rev. Margaret M. Stevens

Would it surprise you to know that according to reliable statistics, more people are attracted to the New Thought philosophy because of their desire for financial abundance than for any other single reason? In the middle of a Sunday message, I once did an impromptu survey, asking those who had come to church for healing to raise their hands. Then those who were seeking solutions for relationship problems. Finally, those who desired greater abundance in their lives. It came as no surprise to me that more than half the congregation raised their hands in response to that last question. That simple inquiry prompted me to announce, then and there, that a new prosperity class would convene the following week. More than a hundred people signed up that very Sunday.

Since that time, prosperity has been the focus of a deep, personal search for answers and practices that work in people's lives, not just to enrich them financially, but to enhance every aspect of their lives. Of course, New Thought's good friend Dr. Catherine Ponder's incredible outpouring of prosperity books over the years has been a tremen-

dous help in that search. As I enter my eighty-first year on this excit-
ing planet, I do so with absolute trust and confidence that the principles and practices for creating abundance developed by Dr. Ponder
and others working in this area do work. My senior years hold no terror or anxiety for me, full as they are of my awareness that God's pro-
vision is constant, dependable, and ever-increasing in all forms of
good—health, happiness, fulfillment, productivity, and peace of mind.

The first pillar in the foundation of a strong, sure prosperity consciousness is the knowledge that prosperity has a spiritual basis, that
God is the source of all supply. Until we know and accept this fact, it
is natural that appearances convince us that some person, some condition, or some investment controls our prosperity or lack of it. It is true
that prosperity works through people and conditions that act as channels, but God is indisputably the one and only source of all supply, all
abundance. Knowing this, we do not panic if people or conditions
seem to let us down financially. We turn instantly to God as the source,
and God guides us to new channels of supply, through people, ideas,
and opportunities that present themselves, sometimes in miraculous,
almost unbelievable ways.

A powerful affirmation that I learned from Dr. Catherine Ponder in
this regard is this: *I do not depend upon persons or conditions for my
prosperity. God is the Source of my supply, and God provides his own
amazing channels of prosperity to me now.* Moses affirmed this truth to
the Hebrew people when he said, "Thou shalt remember the Lord thy
God, for it is He that giveth thee power to get wealth."

Some of the greatest thinkers and demonstrators in New Thought
philosophy have affirmed the spiritual basis of prosperity consciousness. For instance, Ernest Holmes, founder of Religious Science, said:
"God loves a prosperous man/woman," adding, "It is a sin to be poor,
because that condition indicates a belief in separation on the part of
the poor person, an ignorance or misunderstanding of his or her in-
separable Oneness with the source of all supply, God." H. B. Jeffrey, a
prolific writer and influential teacher of truth principles in the early
part of the twentieth century, contributed this brief but potent statement: "It is really stupid to believe in lack." Charles Fillmore, the
cofounder of Unity, wrote: "The Father's desire for us is unlimited

good, not merely the means of a meager existence." And Emma Curtis Hopkins, the "teacher of teachers," wrote in her book *Scientific Christian Mental Practice*: "God is just as much the provider of His children as He is the healer. You must not get mixed up with the idea of poverty any more than the idea of sickness. Persistent thought about prosperity and how prosperity is brought to us will make you a magnet for prosperity. There must be a free giving of your Truth or the world may wait another million years for the wretched poverty of its people to be gone."

The following simple principles have helped me to put these teachings into practice in my life and in the lives of those with whom I have shared them over the past forty years. I heartily and lovingly recommend them.

1. *Faith:* Absolute faith that I am one with the source of all good and that I live in a universal flow of abundance and wholeness.

2. *Good Stewardship:* The right use of resources, good judgment, and wisdom in handling the money that comes into my experience.

3. *Powerful Positive Attitudes:* The daily use of affirmations that lift the consciousness and attract good results. Such practice helps me develop the expectation of good, not necessarily in the form that I might want, but in the form that is for my highest good.

4. *Imaging:* The use of imaging along with affirmations strengthens their effectiveness. I remind myself that the word *desire* in its root means "of the Father." I accept that my deep-seated desires are always divine desires from the Father, seeking expression in my life. Picturing is a prayerful acceptance of those desires. I can picture a thing and bring it through much more quickly and easily than if I try to force it outwardly. I hasten my good by picturing it and myself in the picture.

5. *Tithing:* In my experience, tithing is the real key to prosperity. Ancient people knew that ten was the magic number of increase. The tithe is one-tenth of one's gross income, given freely and lovingly to the channel through which one's good comes into manifestation. Tithing is not charity to one's needy relatives. It is giving back to the source of all good a portion of one's abundance. I have known tithing to start the flow of prosperity in a way that no other single practice has

accomplished. A humorous jingle has helped many people remember the principle: "I no longer strain and strive; I now tithe and thrive."

6. *Gratitude:* I am thankful for every single gift, event, circumstance, and condition that manifests in my life. Is it possible to be thankful for tragedy, hardship, pain, loss, and disappointment? Yes, it is, and thankfulness in all things, as we are advised by St. Paul, allows the conditions in our lives, the good and the not so good, to teach their lessons and move on. Gratitude has opened doors of opportunity for me, revealed hidden blessings in the most unlikely places, and brought a peace of mind and an acceptance of life's hard lessons as nothing else has ever done. Gratitude also includes blessing our prosperity as it flows into our lives, and as it flows out to others to bless and heal them as it has served us. Truly, we live in an incredible flow of divine love and energy that supports and sustains us always and seems to manifest in ever greater ways as we give thanks for it.

I'll close with an affirmation from Dr. Ponder, the woman who has been called "the prophet of prosperity": *I am a divine idea in the mind of God. I am now guided into my true place with the true people and with the true prosperity. I give thanks for a quick and substantial increase in my financial income now.*

By holding this thought and putting these few simple principles into practice, your life can manifest true prosperity in all things, material and spiritual.

MARGARET M. STEVENS was the minister of the Santa Anita Church in Arcadia, California, a non-denominational New Thought church, for twenty-three years. She was also director of the Barnhart School, a fully accredited K–8 day school affiliated with the church, and was founder of the Santa Anita Center for Ministerial Studies and the Association of Independent Churches. Having passed her eightieth birthday, she is in active retirement in Ashland, Oregon, where she hosted the cable television program *The Abundant Life* and recently completed an eight-week series of discussions titled "Age with Passion." She has written both children's and adult books, including *Prosperity Is God's Idea* and *For Families of the Jailed: A Book of Hope.*

Thank You, God,
and Send Me More

Rev. Jerome Stefaniak

Face it. No matter how far you go down the spiritual path, you still have to create money and pay your bills—chop wood and carry water. And sometimes we get so engrossed in the day-to-day scramble that we forget that we are children of an abundant, loving God. We begin to have negative attitudes.

Gratitude is the quickest way to change a negative attitude about life. When you are grateful for the things you currently have, you begin to appreciate what you've already created. When you are grateful for what you already have, the universe begins to supply more.

Remember that the world "out there" is a reflection of our own minds. When we complain and grumble about life, we change from "Christians" into "Mr. Christian" and create a mutiny with our bounty. When we complain, there is no room for the Holy Spirit to work. We are so busy being right about how bad life is, we miss the flowers that are along the path. In fact, we trample them.

Years ago, my teacher, Joe Heaney, had all of us students do a little exercise that turned my thoughts around about money. We were all resentful and grumbling at the time about our financial situations. We were angry at him for having to pay for our classes; we were angry at the city for the electric bills; we were angry at our creditors for always hounding us. In short, we were angry and resentful at everybody, and there wasn't a lot of room for God to work.

One day, Joe had us bring our checkbooks to class. He asked me to open to any page and read off to whom the first check was made out.

"VISA, for fifty dollars."

"And who received the benefits?"

"VISA did."

"No, Jerry, who received the benefits of the services?"

"What do you mean?"

"What did you charge?"

"A couple of dinners, a trip to Hawaii, some clothes."

"So, who received the benefits? Who ate the meals, took the trip, wore the clothes?"

It took me a minute to understand where he was going.

"I received the benefits."

"Good, what's the next check?"

"GMAC—my car payment."

"Who received the benefits of the car?"

"I did."

"The next check?"

"Seattle Power and Light."

"Who received the heating and lighting?"

"I did."

On and on it went. I could not find one check from which I did not *personally* receive some benefit. Every check was written for me! I just didn't want to take responsibility for them. I was so busy blaming the credit card companies, blaming the government, blaming the car industry that I couldn't even receive the gifts that were already mine! I had paid for them, but I had never totally received them.

After that I began to write "thank you" in the memo space of my checks. I still do. At first it wasn't easy. It was amazing how angry and resentful I felt toward the world. It wasn't surprising that my life was full of lack. That's all I acknowledged I had! But after a few checks, I began to smile, and then to laugh. You see, as I wrote "thank you" on each check, my mind automatically reminded me why I was thanking my creditor. "Oh, yeah, Jerry, remember that dinner at the Space Needle? It was nice. And it's nice to have heat and light. And your car does get you around."

What? You have nothing to be thankful for? Are you reading this book? Thank God for being able to see. Can you feel the pages? Thank God for your body. Are you sitting in a nice chair? Thank God for the chair. Are you comfortable? Thank God for your environment. Make thanking God a daily ritual. Thank Him for where you live, the hot shower you take, the breakfast you eat, and the job you have. There were times in my life when all I felt that I could thank God for was a warm shower and my health. But the more I thanked God and others, the more I began to draw to myself. I began to feel abundance, regardless of how my finances looked.

I want to be crystal clear about this change of attitude. Feeling grateful is not just a nice, little New Age exercise you can do. It is not a way to cover over your problems with a veneer of Pollyanna thoughts. Gratitude (along with forgiveness) is one of the most powerful ways of marshalling your love and energy. It actually changes your energetic vibration to a higher frequency. Your body responds physically, shifting from adrenaline to endorphins. From this higher vibration, your attitudes and perceptions about life change. And from there, your life will always change for the better. The Japanese have a saying for this truth: "Appreciation is the highest vibration."

On her audio cassette *Spiritual Madness,* Carolyn Myss tells the story of a man who had a near-death experience. As he floated above his body, an angel asked him whether he would like to see his life from a different perspective. Not knowing any better or what was in store, he said, "Yes. Of course."

What was shown to him were all of the incidents in his life that were hard and troubling. But they were shown from the point of view of what could have happened if only he had shown a little gratitude and appreciation for what he already had. In every case, he got to see beings who wanted to help, but his own self-indulgence and resentment kept them away.

You will never know how close love and help are until you are willing to open up to them, no matter what. And gratitude always opens the heart.

I remember a time, right after I had moved to Houston. I was sitting in a grocery store parking lot with only $2.58 in my pocket. I remember feeling more prosperous than I had ever felt in my life. True, I had no money, but I was surrounded by friends, a new family, and people for whom I cared. I felt rich.

I began to realize that God was always pouring the riches of life onto me, and I was the one wearing a raincoat and holding up an umbrella! I had the thought that night that I could not conceive of how much God wanted to give me. So, I created a little exercise to expand my receiving consciousness. Whenever I create receiving anything, whether it is a penny on the street, a compliment, or a raise, I look to God in my heart and say, "Thank you, God, and send me more."

What this sentence affirms is that I received the gift and that I am open to receiving even more from the universe. So many people will ignore picking up a penny, thinking that a penny does not matter. But they don't realize that the penny represents the part of their minds that is giving them money. If you cannot receive a penny, then you cannot receive a dime, or a dollar, or a raise. Start affirming that you are ready to receive more and more from the universe. And start today.

Another powerful idea is to make a gratitude book. A gratitude book is simply a book that lists everything that you are grateful for: every date you had, all the sex you enjoyed, every gift you received, every sunset. Listing every wonderful thing in your life slowly gets your mind into looking at only the good—at the joy you've already experienced. Right now, my gratitude book lists around five hundred items. And you know what? No matter how badly things are going, I cannot look into my gratitude book without smiling—even just a little. As I once again reap the harvest of those past joys, it lifts me up to realize how rich my life has been and that these things can be experienced again.

When Jesus performed the miracle of feeding five thousand people with a few loaves and fishes, he didn't look down at the food and say, "This will never feed all these people." The first thing he did was to turn his eyes toward heaven and give thanks to his Father. He thanked

God for what he already had and for what he was about to do. Jesus knew that God's universe is an abundant universe. Jesus knew that God is ever-present and just waiting to work through us. Jesus knew that gratitude should be as natural as breathing. Not only was he able to feed five thousand people, but when all the leftovers were collected, there were thirteen baskets full of food remaining.

Do you want to feel better about your life? Do you want to feel what a gift you are to the world? Do you want to see the blessings that are already in your world? Then start by looking at what you already have and say, "Thank you, God, and send me more!"

JEROME STEFANIAK has been a spiritual teacher and breath integration practitioner for twelve years. With his wife, Stavroula Stefaniak, a licensed psychotherapist, he teaches workshops on prosperity, relationships, anger, self-esteem, and sexuality. He also teaches classes in *A Course in Miracles* at Unity Church of Christianity in Houston, Texas. He is the author of *Compassionate Living: Everyday Spirituality* and *Intimacy in Action: Relationships That Feed the Soul.*

Trust the Universe

Rev. Barbara White

Is the universe a friendly place? Albert Einstein once said that how we answer that pivotal question determines the quality of our lives. Personally, Einstein believed that ours is a friendly universe.

Some of us stop trusting the universe because events have hurt us deeply. When traumatic events occur, we may begin to feel that the universe is not a safe place. Instead of believing, as Jesus did, that all good will be added to us, we fear that what we have, what we love, and what we treasure will be taken from us. Instead of an abundant universe, we see a world of lack and limitation, a world that is somehow out to get us. We fear that if life gets too good, surely the other shoe will fall.

Perhaps we fear that God has deserted us or that the dreams of our hearts can never manifest. We go through life comparing ourselves to others, anxious that we'll discover that we are less. Instead of feeling that we are the beloved of life, we feel as though we are life's orphans. Instead of celebrating each day in expectation that all good things will be added to us, we try to get through each day with as little loss and damage as possible. In essence, we believe that the universe may be friendly to a chosen few, but that we are not of that number.

When we get to thinking in this limited and limiting way, we may be confusing the universe—the cosmic world—with the material world. The material world is comprised of people, places, and things that are not always friendly. The human realm of the material world teems with busyness, noise, and confusion. It cannot help but let us down, because humanity is not perfect. The cosmic universe, on the other hand, is always orderly, friendly, and working for our good. Each of us is a vital thread in the cosmic tapestry. No one is expendable, for the universe needs each of us to fulfill its own design. This magnificent universe, this cosmic world, is always doing everything it can to support our success and happiness, so that we can give our gifts to life and shine the unique and radiant light within us.

In this perfectly orchestrated universe, there are no accidents and no mistakes. We have been placed here at this time for a purpose that only we can fulfill. Since we are the way God expresses in this life, the universe must support us. However, the universe can only do *for* us what it can do *through* us. Often our fear, doubt, and anxiety get in the way and block the abundant good that is ours by divine birthright. Unblocking means recognizing that we are the only begotten of the most high God and that we will be maintained, sustained, and carried in abundant life in direct proportion to how fully we recognize this fact, how truly we trust the universe.

Today, let's lay down our burden of worry and trust that the universe is constantly working on our behalf. If we allow ourselves to fear that life is passing us by, it will! Instead, let's get up each day willing to trust and serve life through our willingness to help others, through our kindness, love, and compassion. Let our prayer each morning be: "Dear God (or Life or Universe), how can I serve you today?" Then we show up and do our best to be a blessing to all we encounter, knowing and affirming that we are in league with an Infinite Power and Presence in whom all things are possible.

Ernest Holmes, the founder of Religious Science, once said, "When we learn to trust the Universe, we shall be happy, joyous, and free." So let us learn to relax, trust more, fear less, and be of service, because the truth is that all is well, because God is right where we are. Let us trust that our hearts' desires will be fulfilled, not always in our time frame, but in the fullness of the universe's blessings. We are life's precious gift to itself, incredibly magnificent beings. Let's breathe that in, walk with our heads held high knowing that God is always doing for us what we could never even dream of doing for ourselves and that God is a trustworthy benefactor.

When we put our hand in the hand of the Infinite and trust the universe, our lives change and grow in a most magnificent way. When we believe that life has meaning and purpose, we understand that God has ordained for each of us a place of unfoldment, a means for us to serve as the ears, eyes, mouth, and heart of God to all we meet.

The desires of our hearts were placed there by God. Someday we will be able to see how all the different pieces of where we've been, what we've done, and what we've experienced fit together to make a perfect whole. When we trust the universe and show up every day to be of service, an abundant life cannot help but be ours. All we need do is have faith in the process!

BARBARA WHITE is senior minister of the Downey Church of Religious Science in Downey, California. She serves on the faculty of the Holmes Institute in Los Angeles. A regular contributor to *Science of Mind Magazine,* she has been a guest panelist on the television show *Taking Charge of Your Life.*

The Magic of Acceptance

Dr. Roger W. Teel

Have you ever experienced the frustration of offering someone a gift that they refused to accept?

Consider that Jesus declared, "It is the Father's good pleasure to give you the Kingdom." You are offered blessings for everyday living that are far greater than you might imagine. All the good of God is available to you, but it can't come into your life unless you have your "welcome mat" out. As Dr. Ernest Holmes writes, "It is the nature of the universe to give us what we are able to take. It cannot give us more. It has given all, yet we have not accepted the greater gifts."

It is often quite revealing to ask yourself, "How am I doing at accepting the Kingdom of All-Good I have been offered?"

To help answer this question, Jesus offered the parable of the wedding feast. In this story, a king has arranged for the marriage of his son. Though the king has sent out invitations and prepared a lavish banquet, when it was time for the wedding, no one came. Twice the king's servants went out to remind people, but the servants came back with the news that the guests who had been invited were too busy to attend.

The Kingdom of All-Good offered to each of us by the infinite presence and power of God is much like a bountiful wedding feast. There is food for a hungry mind, love and support for all our seasons and situations, answers to every problem, strength for those who feel weary, hope for the discouraged, confidence and peace of mind for the distressed, and growth and abundance of all kinds. And everyone is invited. But like the king's guests, we get busy and distracted. Though the truths that could keep our lives inwardly growing and outwardly prospering have been known for ages, all too often we refuse to attend the feast and look instead for superficial sources of satisfaction. Yet, inevitably, especially in times of change and challenge, we find ourselves hungering for true empowerment, for the inner nourishment that keeps our lives healing and growing.

The inner feast to which we have been invited is the experience of connecting, of unifying with the wellspring of God-Life. Making that connection opens up the flow of divine qualities latent within everyone. The feast of God is awareness-expanding and life-altering. As we evolve our awareness by partaking in greater spiritual understanding, everything else in life prospers as well.

Let me play the role of the king's servant and remind you of his generous invitation. Let me invite you to come to the feast . . . right now.

A key step in the process of accepting God's invitation is to "make the mold"—to hold an image that is the mental equivalent of our desires. A story in a major newspaper told of an elderly man who was poor in resources but rich in spirit. The sidewalk in front of his house was a broken mess and dangerous to use. He deeply desired to have a new sidewalk that went right up to his porch. So, he prayed: "God, this is unacceptable. I know it is your good pleasure to give me everything I can accept. I accept a new sidewalk, and this is the final word on it."

Soon after, the man had his children haul away the pieces of broken concrete. He found some old boards in his backyard and made a form for the new sidewalk. When this was in place, he said, "OK, God, I've done my part."

About ten days later, a cement truck was barreling down the man's street. It tried to make the turn at the corner, but it tipped over. No one was hurt, but the workers had to dump the cement quickly before it hardened in the truck. The elderly gentleman simply walked onto his porch, pointed to the waiting forms, and proclaimed, "You can put that cement right there. Thank you, God!"

It's not our business to know how the universe is going to assist us. Our task of acceptance is to create a clear and vibrant mental image into which the universe can pour its limitless substance.

In the second part of the parable of the wedding feast, the king commanded his servants to go out and find anybody available to fill the tables at the feast. Much to the king's delight, his banquet hall became full of guests. As he surveyed the gathering, the king noticed one person who was not dressed appropriately. He condemned this person and had him thrown out.

Just as we clothe our bodies, we "dress" our minds with garments that reflect the prevailing patterns of our thoughts. Like the poorly dressed man at the king's feast, the attitudes we sometimes wear are not appropriate for enjoying God's good. Many, for instance, wear the rags of unworthiness: "It's too good to be true." "There's not enough for me." "It's my lot in life never to prosper." These thoughts are unwelcome guests at the banquet.

We are the principal authorities in our awareness, and, like the king, we must be ready to deal vigorously with these unsuitable aspects of our thinking. Though throwing the unwelcome guests out is one solution, the highest and best thing for us to do is to embrace these parts of ourselves and dress them in more suitable clothes, thereby lifting them to a higher level of acceptance.

During a class I taught several years ago, a man I knew shared that he had lost his job and desperately needed a new one. When the class took a break, I sat down with him. The man told me that he didn't have a lot of savings. I asked if he had been interviewing, and he said, "Oh, yes, I went to five interviews today and was turned down every time."

I asked him how he was dealing with being turned down, and he admitted he was getting discouraged. I then asked if he had a clear idea about the job he was looking for, what he wanted both to give and receive in employment. He said that he did, but his discouragement was mounting as were his doubts about himself and his skills.

It seemed clear to me that this man had "made the mold" in that he had a clear idea about the job he wanted to find. Yet, his discouragement and doubts were like unsuitable guests who had shown up at the promised feast. In support, I tried to help the man find more suitable garments for his "guests."

"Remember," I told him, "divine love in you is more powerful than fear. Remember your job image and allow your passion for it to grow. You'll soon find that your passion can overwhelm the fear.

"Now, about those turndowns. You are going to have to experience a certain number of 'no's before you get to your 'yes.' I'm not sure how many, but I want to congratulate you, because you eliminated five of them today! You might get four or five more 'no's tomorrow, but you should greet them with a sense of accomplishment, because they mean that you're even further down the path toward your goal."

The man's face brightened at these words, and he appeared to be newly energized.

Three weeks later, the man shared with the class that, despite being turned down day after day, he had kept his passion fueled and the image of the job he wanted firmly in his mind. By believing that every day he was moving closer to his goal, he had outfitted his fear in a proper garment for the feast. Then one day he walked into an office for an interview, and the job that the woman behind the desk had available so perfectly suited the man that she said simply, "Where have you been all this time?"

Create the mold, deal with unwelcome visitors by transforming them, and keep on cooperating with the all-giving power of life. Remember also to accept the "first gifts" of God, which are the inner gifts given spontaneously and immediately when you accept the invitation to the feast. They'll come flooding forth even before the "cement truck has tipped over," even before you walk into the right person's office. These gifts include encouragement, peace, a sense of hope and purpose, and a feeling of love and compassion for others and for yourself. Accept these gifts as you journey toward the feast.

Finally, remember that some gifts are priceless. A mother had gone through a divorce and felt overwhelmed by lingering pain, depression, and sleeplessness. The day of her birthday came, but she had no desire to celebrate. When she came home from work, however, she found that her seven-year-old daughter and seventeen-year-old son had prepared a birthday cake and presents for her.

The mother made an effort and opened a few of the presents. As she and the children were eating the cake, the seven-year-old said, "Mommy, I've got another present for you. Close your eyes and hold out your hand."

The mother did so. She felt her daughter's little hand touch her palm.

"OK, Mommy, you can open your eyes!"

When the mother opened her eyes, her palm seemed empty. She looked at her daughter with questioning eyes.

The little girl smiled and said, "Mommy, the gift is happiness."

At that moment, a weight lifted from the mother's heart. She smiled at her children and opened to the gifts of the universe that had come to her through the hand of a child.

We, too, have such gifts available to us. We have only to open our hearts to the magic of acceptance.

Part III

Creative Endeavors

Introduction: Heaven's Kiss of Inspiration

Dr. Michael Beckwith

Divine inspiration is that "certain something" that distinguishes works of creative genius. In the movie *Amadeus,* you'll recall that the composer Antonio Salieri went mad in his jealous efforts to possess and destroy Mozart's creative spirit. But in that film and in our own experience, that which is infused with the immortal breath of inspiration can never die! While creative expressions born solely of the surface of the mind last only until fickle humanity discards them as passé, the simplest creative act kissed by inspiration endures.

What secret did those great creative geniuses of spirit, art, science, and literature possess? What did Jesus, Buddha, George Washington Carver, Hildegard of Bingen, Einstein, Emerson, Rilke, Bach, and other illumined ones share that helped their works to stir our souls? It is simply this: *Inspiration flows into individual consciousness through the soul faculty of intuition.* As we read in John 15:4: "The branch cannot bear fruit of itself, except it abide in the vine." When we drink the wine of inspiration flowing through the soul's intuitive communion with the divine, we taste the rich fruit of conscious creativity.

The key that unlocks the storehouse of inspired creativity lies within our own beings. We tune it through the sweet disciplines of meditation, affirmative prayer, and mindfulness. These practices sensitize our consciousness to answer inspiration's knock, for, as it is written in Revelation 3:20: "Behold, I stand at the door and knock. If anyone hears My voice and opens the door, I will come in to him and dine with him, and he with Me."

True creativity, then, flows from a divine source. Look around you at the bountiful creations of nature, and you'll understand instantly why this is so. To create is to cause something to come into existence. The causative power that operates within an individual consciousness reflects the causative principle through which the universe itself came into being—the first cause, the divine principle of creativity. As we come more and more to discern spiritually and to celebrate the divine source of all creative production, our own creative process comes to reflect the work of the divine, and we begin to participate in conscious creativity.

I discovered our intuitive gift for connecting with divine inspiration for myself when, as a young seeker, I conferred through recurring dreams with Johann Sebastian Bach. Now, I wasn't exactly a Bach groupie, so naturally I wondered why Johann was hanging out in my dream state instead of Jimi Hendrix! But there I was, dialoguing with Mr. Bach, asking him how to create sacred music that would call forth my highest creative potential and release the inner splendor within its listeners.

These dreams stayed filed away in my memory bank until some years later when I began my musical collaboration with Rickie Byars, music director of the Agape International Choir. Then I realized the deeper significance and practical nature of these nocturnal dialogues. Rickie and I regularly commune with the divine originator of inspiration through meditation and prayer. Individually and collectively it has been consistently revealed to us that the creative and intellectual self can be flooded with inspiration that directs the orchestration and everything else necessary to create lyrics and music that uplift, transform, and heal.

I have also come to recognize that the universe has a keen sense of humor and that insight sometimes occurs on the installment plan. So I was not surprised, recently, when I came across a passage in Arthur M. Abell's *Talks with Great Composers* that seemed to explain why Bach had entered my dreams: "Where there is devotional music," said Bach, "God is always at hand with His gracious presence." The great Johannes Brahms put it this way: "I will tell you about my method of communicating with the Infinite, for all truly inspired ideas come from God. I begin by appealing directly to my Maker, and straight-away the ideas flow in upon me, directly from God. . . . You see, the powers from which all truly great composers . . . drew their inspiration is the same power that enabled Jesus to work his miracles."[1] Once again we are given to realize that "in-spiration" is an inside job!

Why this is so is not difficult to understand. Thought, the forerunner of action, is a vibrational energy that creates form in its own likeness. In the absolute, every thought and act is creative. Indigenous cultures have always understood this. To this day, through prayer and ritual, native peoples call on the Spirit of Creativity present in all things. Moreover, the creativity at the heart of all things is not limited to artistic endeavors. The Buddhist teachings on "mindfulness" that call us to consciousness of the present moment powerfully express the realization that creativity courses through even the simplest of actions. The practice of mindful walking, for example, makes each step a creative act that reveals the ecstasy of inspired perfection within every footfall. As the revered Zen master Thich Nhat Hanh teaches: "If we take steps without anxiety, in peace and joy, then we will cause a flower to bloom on the Earth with every step."[2]

To the Western materialist mind-set so prevalent in our "high tech–low touch" culture, the practice of Buddhist mindfulness no doubt seems impractical. Many popular books on time management urge us to use our downtime to create more lists, call our brokers on our cell phones, contact clients, and make maximum use of each moment

[1] Arthur M. Abell, *Talks with Great Composers* (New York: Citadel, 1994), 16, 74.
[2] Thich Nhat Hanh, *Present Moment, Wonderful Moment* (California: Parallax Press, 1990), 58.

to make another dollar. Live this way, and the body runs through the paces while the Spirit is absent from the creative benefits of mindful walking, cooking, gazing, driving, or simply sitting. The conscious creativity of mindfulness calls on us to stop! And breathe! It asks us to hear that we are not to live in an atmosphere of frantic competition, but of mindful and conscious creativity!

Stillness itself is a creative act, for in a state of inward listening, we may intuit the still, small voice announcing its presence, revealing its vision of inspired creative expression. Within an instant a breakthrough may occur. The primordial sound of creation's cosmic vibration—the *Aum* of the Vedas, the *Hum* of the Tibetans, the *Amen* of the Judeo-Christians, and the *Amin* of the Muslims—may flood us with a surge of divine inspiration beyond description.

So, when we talk about conscious creativity, we tread on sacred ground, the holy ground upon which we weave the tapestry of our lives. Created by an inherent causative principle within individual consciousness, our lives as well as our artistic creations take on the texture of that divine center around which our consciousness revolves. When we set aside time each day for deep communion with the infinite, then, as surely as day follows night, the light of inspiration will illuminate our beings.

In the essays in this section, conscious creativity is explored from many levels of awareness. They demonstrate that divine inspiration speaks, writes, composes, sings, parents, invents, loves, illumines, liberates, and makes us its instruments.

May your incarnation be an inspired journey of wakefulness, mindfulness, peace, and bliss, and may heaven's kiss of inspiration be upon your brow.

MICHAEL BECKWITH is founder and senior minister of the Agape International Center of Truth in Culver City, California, a vibrant center of New Thought activity, with 7,000 members and 19,000 friends in metropolitan Los Angeles, New York, Brazil, South Africa, and Jamaica. He oversees a network of twenty ministries, including those that feed the homeless, serve prisoners and their families, provide hospice grief support, and facilitate a twenty-four-hour prayer phone line. He is director of the Los Angeles campus of the Holmes Institute, a founding member of the Association for Global New Thought, a national codirector of "A Season for Nonviolence," and a frequent speaker at national and international conferences.

The Song Inside Us

Sage Bennet, Ph.D.

To be spiritual is to create.
ERNEST HOLMES

I remember a story my mother used to tell. At a kindergarten Christmas play, a group of children were on stage singing a song. Something went wrong with the stage management, and before the song was over, the curtain fell in front of the children. The audience could hear a mixture of giggles, tears, and confusion from behind the curtain. Then a little girl found her way through the curtain onto the stage, finished singing the song, and disappeared behind the curtain.

I was that little girl.

I don't remember doing this, but I do remember being a child singing with all my heart as I played. I remember my natural connection with the spontaneous playfulness of God where all is possible, delightful, and fun. I believe this spontaneous connection with the infinite stream of creative energy—God, Life, or Divine Presence—is available all the time.

I think we each have a song to sing. Call it life purpose, service, or the work we came here to do. We already have this song inside us, and it calls us to sing. At times we may give in to our fears of not having enough talent, time, or money. Yet we notice, time and again, that divine melodies still rise from our depths. We come to realize that the song inside us—in its simplicity, subtle beauty, and innocent purity—is stronger than any limiting belief.

Perhaps as children we had less cultural conditioning to keep us from connecting with the endless stream of creativity that it is our birthright to tap. As we mature and move from play to work, we may stiffen in our posture. We begin to dismiss spontaneous glimmers of new ideas as immature, frivolous, and something we don't have time for. We may too readily believe that the experts know better than we do, or that being an artist or a genius is for the rare and seldom chosen. We close down to the wisdom and excitement of our innate creativity.

Nevertheless, our creative genius awaits our acknowledgment. I think the great nineteenth-century poet and essayist Ralph Waldo Emerson was right when he pointed out in "Self-Reliance" that many people do not claim the creative genius within: "In every work of genius we recognize our own rejected thoughts: they come back to us with a certain alienated majesty."

I have seen college students destroy beautiful stories and artwork because they devalued rather than honored their talents. I have seen friends paint beautiful canvasses only to hide them in basements erroneously dooming them to amateur status. In contrast, I have seen third-graders shine brilliantly, and even amaze their teachers, when they are invited to put on imaginary "genius caps."

By believing in our creative potential, we can expand our creativity. First we have to allow ourselves to be open. Then we can catch the vision of the spiritual pattern of perfection within that is waiting to be revealed as our lives. Nature and art are full of examples of this process. The acorn contains the potential of the towering oak tree. Michelangelo envisioned the Sistine Chapel in his mind as a fully formed masterpiece before he began to paint.

While putting together ideas for this essay, I had a dream. In my dream, a man in prison, sick and tired of life, was dying from self-inflicted wounds. Prison officials called in a minister to speak to the man and to offer a prayer. In a soft and loving voice, the minister told the man what she saw: that he was a being of love and beauty with a purpose in life.

At that moment, the prisoner caught a glimpse of himself as an artist. He saw himself sculpting beautiful images of freedom—birds in flight, ocean waves, horses galloping in the surf. This vision so filled him with inspiration that his wounds healed and his spirit was freed. In the next scene of the dream, an artist who had once been in prison was being honored at the opening of a sculpture exhibition called "Images of Freedom."

I see myself in all parts of the dream. Perhaps you do, too. When I am disconnected from my creative source, I feel like a prisoner, in hopeless despair, dying of self-inflicted wounds. Yet I also see that desperation often opens me to the revelation of a new truth about myself. In the dream, when I was ready to die to my old self, I created an opening for my artist self to emerge—the part of me that is devoted to creating and experiencing freedom. When I connect to this inner imperative to fulfill my creative purpose, I am truly set free.

Though one part of me identified with the prisoner, another part of me, depicted in the dream as the minister, knew my true, spiritual identity. Once I shifted perspective to this spiritual identity, I glimpsed my creative purpose, which healed my old wounds and provided focus for my life purpose.

I think this dream has something to say to us all. There is a divine idea within each of us that wants to express itself as our lives. It may express as forms of art—music, poetry, photography, paintings, prose, theater, and song. It may express as art forms in living—health, loving relationships, consistent spiritual practice, and meaningful work. When we catch the vision of our creative purpose, our creative expression flows forth as naturally as the seed that is planted in fertile earth bursts forth in flower. At our core we are spiritual beings connected to the infinite creativity of God.

We are each here to sing our song.

Just Do It

Dr. Florence B. Phillips

JUST DO IT are three powerful, dynamic, almost magical words that can empower us to take on just about anything we want to accomplish. JUST DO IT helps us take action when we hesitate to try something new or different. Acting on the JUST DO IT principle propels us to move rather than freeze with fear, to leap rather than teeter on the proverbial fence of indecision.

It is so easy to sit on the sidelines and let life pass us by. We whine and complain, argue for our limitations, and mutter about how much better someone else can do something. Yet, many times, when the thing we chose not to do because of our insecurity is done by someone else, we look at it and say with consternation, "I could have done better than that!" while our inner committee shouts, "But you didn't!"

I readily admit that until I started heeding the JUST DO IT command, I was inclined to procrastinate or be just plain timid about launching out. I have come to understand that Spirit would not be prodding me into action if my abilities were not already wrapped up in the new creation, just waiting to be revealed. When the urge to move forward struggles to overcome my natural tendency to hold back, I feel Spirit saying, "I want to express through you in this way, Beautiful Godling, so let's get going!"

At such moments, I like to bring to mind two occasions when I heeded the urging of my inner committee to JUST DO IT, and everything changed. The first was at the end of World War II when my husband returned from overseas. He chose to take advantage of the chance to get a college education being offered to the returning veterans under the G.I. Bill. I planned to get a secretarial position to supplement our income, since I had been thoroughly conditioned to believe I was too stupid to consider higher education for myself.

But Spirit had plans for me. It sent several friends who recognized the potential that I could not see. Their encouragement pierced my bubble of self-doubt and led me to take college entrance exams. With my inner committee yelling JUST DO IT, I took the plunge. You cannot imagine my surprise when I learned I was, in fact, quite a good candidate. With the words JUST DO IT ringing in my ears, I reasoned, "If I find I can't cut it, no sweat. I'll just go about this challenge like a clock—one tick at a time." To my amazement, I graduated with honors, my academic record proving that my early programming had been sorely inaccurate.

The second time JUST DO IT changed my life came when my husband and I evolved out of our orthodox thinking into New Thought. Since he found he could no longer preach the traditional doctrine, Spirit led him to look into becoming a Religious Science minister. He enrolled in the School of Ministry in Los Angeles. The dean of the school, Dr. Al Lowe, became an angel of Spirit to me as well, once again breaking through my doubts and challenging me to enter the course of study as well.

My first reaction to Dr. Lowe's suggestion was, "Who me? A minister? My five brothers would really find that a hoot!" But once again, my inner committee shouted JUST DO IT. With a what-have-I-got-to-lose attitude, I decided to take a chance and see what God wanted to do through me. As a result of that decision, my husband and I have walked the path of ministry together since 1976.

The steadier my steps became, the more chances life gave me to build my confidence by trying new things. I found I could make ball gowns that equaled many I had seen on the store mannequins. I could tastefully decorate our home—and even the church—without relying on someone else's say-so. I dared to cook for crowds. One time, with a limited musical background, I even directed our small choir in a Christmas cantata.

When it found a willing student, the JUST DO IT inner committee really went to work overtime. When I found myself floating through the silent sky about a thousand feet above the earth in a hot-air balloon, it had almost pushed the envelope too far. And, when my husband got his private pilot's license and wanted me to fly with him in the rocky, little Cessna aircraft, I had to put my foot down and let the committee know it was being too pushy. I still have choice, and there are some things I just choose not to do.

One lesson I have really gotten is that we are never saved once and for all from the errors of our false assumptions. I am still learning "I'm beautiful and capable of being the best me I can be." My abilities are already wrapped up in my possibilities, but now the inner committee has to be called into session less and less to goad me into action.

As I take each flying leap and JUST DO IT, Spirit comforts me with the deep assurance that whatever is needed to make things work out—time, energy, wisdom, patience, or money—will be given to me in time and on time. Then, all the vitality of the universe rushes in to assist me.

Spirit constantly reminds me that each of us has within us a power greater than we are that is at our command and joyously wants to see us through anything we choose to do. Our part is just to step out and sprinkle our unique talents and abilities into the world like gentle snowflakes, believing in ourselves as others have believed in us.

Now that my once fragile wings are stronger, I find that the more I JUST DO IT, the more confidence I have in myself. I congratulate myself for my willingness to allow divine energy to express as me with my own unique talents and abilities. Each time I take off and JUST DO IT, I feel another layer of my true self being unveiled and another facet of my inner splendor revealing itself as a blessing in my world.

It is never too late to start believing in yourself and to allow your unique, talented, lovable snowflakes gently to embrace your world with blessings. Don't hold back! Stand tall! Get off the dime! JUST DO IT!

FLORENCE B. PHILLIPS is co-minister of the Palm Springs Church of Religious Science in Palm Springs, California. A former high school English teacher, she is a frequent contributor to *Science of Mind Magazine*. She has developed and facilitated workshops in Spiritual Mind Treatment, meditation, prosperity, and *A Course in Miracles*.

With God All Things Are Possible

Rev. Claudia C. Stachowski

Who do you think you are?" "Where are you going to get the money?" "Who's going to do all the work?" Those questions raised by some members of my church probably sound familiar if you have ever tried to share a dream or to step out and follow your heart toward some creative endeavor.

I am a New Thought minister and a full-time public school speech therapist. It is no coincidence that the name of my ministry is Center of the Living Word. My deep love for New Thought and for the spoken word came together a little more than a year ago in the dream of hosting a well-known speaker whose message could have a profound and lasting influence on my community. As my dream took shape, those questions rang in my ears, triggering a wave of self-doubt.

I had first realized the impact positive words could have while working with children in my speech groups. I remember an occasion when one child in the group was trying, with limited success, to pronounce a certain word. In response, another child chimed in with the words I always use to encourage effort: "Nice try." "Remember how hard that used to be?" "Wow, I can tell you are really trying!" Children, I realized, are like little mirrors, reflecting back what they see, what they hear, and how they are treated. Words of encouragement make a profound difference.

The inherent kindness and helpfulness of children who have been exposed to adult encouragement also became apparent the year my school district decided to bring severely handicapped children into the neighborhood schools rather than sending them to special schools. The building where I taught would house four children with very different needs: two five-year-old girls, one profoundly deaf and the other a spastic quadriplegic; a five-year-old noncommunicative, potentially autistic boy; and a ten-year-old boy with multiple handicaps. I viewed their arrival as a marvelous opportunity to teach all of the children to accept differences.

Once again, the children rose to the occasion. During the six years that these special children attended my school, I never once heard a cruel or unkind word spoken about any of them. On the contrary, the "regular" children took them under their wings, protected them, and encouraged each of them. I am convinced that this was so because of the example set by the adults.

This realization that children imitate the adults in their lives helped me to see how my dream of hosting a well-known speaker might manifest. I was listening one day to a tape about Arun Gandhi, the grandson of Mahatma Gandhi, and about the grassroots movement he had started called "A Season for Nonviolence." Gandhi began this project as a living memorial to two men who gave their lives for the practice of nonviolence, Mahatma Gandhi and Dr. Martin Luther King, Jr. A spark was lit in me at that moment that grew into a fire of passion to do something proactive toward establishing peace. And what better place to start than with children? With Arun Gandhi's help, my school could be immersed in the language and practice of nonviolence and acceptance.

The dreams that God places in our hearts are like puzzle pieces; they fit somewhere, but not always in the space we originally think they belong. It sometimes takes time and trial and error before a piece fits into its right and perfect place. This was what happened with my dream of hosting a speaker. The perfect place for the speaker, I realized, was with the children, not just with my congregation. Children are the future, and if we dream of creating a peaceful world, we must teach them.

Once I had made the proper connections, my dream took on a life all its own. Ideas came quickly, which was a good thing, because if I had had the time to think, I might have allowed limiting thoughts and self-doubting questions to talk me right out of my dream. But something miraculous was happening, and I just kept following the nudges and guidance I was given.

Within two weeks' time, my idea was accepted as our school theme for the following year, and I had written a proposal to my school district requesting that it fund my trip to the task force planning meeting for "A Season for Nonviolence" at the Living Enrichment Center in Portland, Oregon. My proposal was accepted, and all my travel expenses were paid.

Shortly after my return, I was inspired to invite Arun Gandhi to speak to both my elementary school and my congregation. The administration of my school district supported me in theory but were not able to supply additional funding. So, one night in prayer, I pulled out the "God Can" I had purchased from the bookstore at the Living Enrichment Center. The "God Can" helps a person remember that nothing is impossible with God. I wrote on a slip of paper words telling Spirit that if this project were mine to do, if it were God's will, I was willing to do my part. Then, I let it go completely and took one step at a time guided by that familiar nudge from within.

Some doors opened, while others slammed in my face. At first, as doors closed, my response would be anger or frustration. But when I reminded myself that this was God's project, I would cool down and say, "OK, God, what now?" As work on the project progressed, I got really good at this, and each time a door closed, I would cool down more quickly, ask God for help sooner, and trust that an even bigger and wider door would soon open. Not only was enough money donated to cover all the expenses, but I also met many people who volunteered their services.

One day while shopping for snowshoes, I was guided to begin a conversation with another shopper, and as one thing led to another, she volunteered to serve as a professional photographer to chronicle the event. A local optometrist who had heard about the event also volunteered to take photos. The day I came home and found a message from the host of a local television program who offered to cover the event I was like a giddy schoolgirl. Then the mayor's office called offering its support, and my delight had no bounds, especially since I had done nothing to make those contacts.

In the end, Arun and his wife, Sunanda Gandhi, spent five days in our community speaking about the principles of nonviolence to a variety of audiences. They spoke at my elementary school in the suburbs, at a culturally diverse school in the city, and at three middle schools. They gave a community lecture, and, oh, yes, Arun was the guest speaker for a Sunday service at my church.

The next time that voice inside your head asks, "Who do think you are?" your answer should be, "I am a child of God. With God, all things are possible."

CLAUDIA C. STACHOWSKI is the minister of Center of the Living Word in Clarence, New York. She is also a public school speech and language pathologist who has contributed to the textbook *Speech and Language* and is a frequent presenter at educational conferences and workshops in the field of speech pathology. She was the task force leader for "A Season for Nonviolence" in New York State.

A New Way to Work

Rev. Wendy Craig-Purcell

People today expect much more from work than their grandparents did. To previous generations, work was a means to an end. If the typical forty-hour workweek provided the resources to buy a home, put food on the table, clothe the family, and possibly pay for college, that was enough. Whether the work was enjoyable did not have the same importance as it does to us. Today, in addition to financial rewards, we expect our work to provide a creative outlet, satisfaction, self-expression, and personal growth. Sadly, few of us have discovered how to achieve all that.

Some people are fortunate to be in careers they enjoy, with people they like and an environment that is positive. But what can you do if this fortunate circumstance is not yours? Is your only hope winning the lottery or marrying into money? Or, must you change jobs to find the satisfaction you seek?

Perhaps the answer is changing the way you think about work. Consider for a moment the possibility that the opposite of "hard work" is not leisure or play, but rather investing yourself fully in whatever you're doing at the moment. Consider the possibility that when you understand this truth, you'll discover that your greatest joy is not what you do apart from work, but rather what you do while you're working.

In *The Book of Virtues*, William Bennett invites this kind of thinking about work when he writes: "What are you going to be when you grow up? is a question about work. What is your work in the world going to be? What will be your works? These are not fundamentally questions about jobs and pay, but questions about life. . . . Work in this fundamental sense is not what we do for a living but what we do with our living."[1]

Seen rightly, work provides the greatest opportunity for personal growth, self-discovery, and creative expression. Actually, whatever your job, the most important thing you "produce" at work is yourself. Nineteenth-century social reformer John Ruskin expressed this truth when he wrote: "The highest reward for a man's toil is not what he gets for it but what he becomes by it."

I discovered this truth for myself when my congregation kept outgrowing its temporary meeting spaces. It seemed clear it was time to work toward building a permanent home for the church that would be large enough to accommodate growth. Early into our building program, prosperity teacher Edwene Gaines told me pointedly, "Honey, you're not building a building! You're building consciousness—your consciousness and the congregation's. When that consciousness is built, you'll have your building." Edwene was absolutely right, of course. The work of building a church has as much to do with building people as it does with bricks, mortar, and glass.

This new understanding of the nature of work is radically different from the notion we grew up with. Viewing work as something we do merely for external rewards blocks our ability to see a task as something worth doing for its own sake. When we think only about how much we're being paid, work becomes something we get through so that we can get on with our "real" lives.

Let me illustrate. An old man was being teased by a group of neighborhood children. No amount of persuasion or anger could stop them.

---

[1] Bennett, William, *The Book of Virtues* (New York: Simon and Schuster, 1993), 347.

So the man tried a different tactic. He offered to pay the children a dollar each if they would return on Tuesday and insult him again. Tuesday came, and the children showed up to shout the same insults and claim their money. The man then told the children that if they returned on Wednesday, he'd pay them a quarter. On Wednesday, they returned, insulted the man again, and collected their quarters. Then the man informed the children that Thursday's rate would be just a penny. "Forget it," the children said. They never taunted the man again.

In addition to understanding that work has intrinsic value, we can also benefit from a new commitment to the quality of work we produce. Taking pride in our work is a simple, effective way to regain a sense of creative mastery and increase the personal satisfaction work can bring.

My husband, John, and I love antiques. For my ordination, John bought me a seventeenth-century English grandfather clock. Crafted of mahogany and intricately inlaid with walnut, the clock is a work of art that still keeps time beautifully. Engraved into the elegant brass face of the clock is the name "Nathaniel Plummer Wellington"—the man who made it. Judging from the clock's beauty and precision, Wellington must have taken tremendous pride in his work, so much so that he quite literally put his name on it.

Is the same true for you? Do you consistently turn out work you're proud to "put your name on"? Or have you been content with doing only what you have to until you find the job you really want where you'll be willing to give your all? Withholding our best because we don't like the job we have or the people we work for is a common way we sabotage ourselves. We justify our actions by saying: "I'll give more when they appreciate me more." "I'll do better when everyone else does." "I'll do more when they pay me more." Imagine for a moment that, like Nathaniel Plummer Wellington, people will know you only by the work you do. If this were so, what would people know of you? Is this how you want to be known?

It's time to stop making excuses and to understand that no matter who signs your paycheck, you're really working for yourself. Whatever your job, your work can be a creative endeavor and a spiritual practice that reminds you not to hold back but to create something that reflects the best of what you are—not for anyone's sake but your own.

The irony is that when you work for yourself, you are always well rewarded. Consider my friend Tom. After being trained in videography, Tom looked for a job in Hollywood but found that no one was hiring. No matter how many times he heard, "We have no openings," his desire wasn't thwarted. Deciding he might as well go for broke and "apply" where he really wanted to work, Tom approached *Entertainment Tonight* and offered to work without pay for six months. After that time, if they were pleased with the quality of his work, they could hire him. They did. Tom has worked for the show for almost twenty years now.

When you consistently produce excellent work and are willing to give of yourself, something miraculous happens. You wind up feeling better about yourself, and that feeling of pride can't help but have a positive impact on your life. And, because the universe works according to principle, one of two additional things may happen: Either the environment around you changes so you'll be rightly compensated where you are, or you'll have earned the right to be somewhere else, and the universe will open a new door and provide a better opportunity.

Even on the greatest of jobs, there are usually aspects we don't like. This challenge, too, provides us with an opportunity to stretch and grow. Rather than finding someone else to do those difficult tasks, or putting them off until the last minute, or not doing them at all and hoping we don't get caught, we might approach the parts of a job we like least from a creative and playful angle.

Remember Mark Twain's clever boy hero Tom Sawyer? Aunt Polly assigned Tom the job of whitewashing the fence. It was a sunny summer day, and Tom wanted to be playing, not painting. But he had an idea. Knowing that his friends would soon come walking down the street, he decided to make the work of whitewashing look like fun. He started whistling as he painted designs on the fence and then filled them in, admiring his work all the while. Soon, all his friends not only wanted to "play" at painting the fence, but they were offering to pay Tom for the privilege of doing so!

Finally, it's important to squeeze all the good—all the learning—out of the work that's right in front of you whether or not it's your "perfect" work. When aspiring actor Scott Glenn (you'll remember him from the films *The Silence of the Lambs, The Hunt for Red October,* and *Backdraft*) was sixteen, he went to Los Angeles to pursue his dream. One of his first jobs was removing the rust from water tanks on the top of buildings thirty stories high and then painting them. In the beginning, he was so scared that his hands shook so badly he could barely do the work. To overcome his fear, he focused completely on the rust, working to remove every spot. His strategy worked. What was true of his youthful endeavors is still Scott's career philosophy: "To do your best, it's necessary to concentrate fully and avoid distraction. If you do, it's amazing what you can accomplish."

Sometimes we're so busy looking ahead and considering where we are as a stepping stone to where we want to be that we miss the creative and spiritual richness of the task right in front of us.

Control Your Mind

Dr. David J. Walker

What would you do if you sat on a tack?

1. Complain about the pain?
2. Ignore the pain?
3. Resent the tack?
4. Resent the person who put it there?
5. Resent yourself for choosing that seat?
6. Expect the tack to move away by itself?
7. Remove the tack?

If you chose number seven, you can change your life! Why? Because changing your life is determined by your ability to do what is necessary. When it comes to sitting on tacks, most people know what to do. Can you say the same about the rest of your life? You don't change your life for the better by complaining, ignoring, resenting, or expecting life to change by itself. You change your life by taking control.

Everyone wants to be in control of what is happening to them. This is natural and healthy because it reflects an awareness of your creative power. After a while, however, it becomes obvious that the control that needs to be exercised is not over people or circumstances; it's over your own mind.

And so, changing your life for the better takes doing! Actually, doing comes second. Knowing comes first. When it comes to changing your life, what is there to know? First, you must know that you *can!* The reason you can is that the creative power that energizes all of life exists at its highest level within the human mind. What a great start! You can accomplish what you set out to do because your very nature as a spiritual being is creative.

The second thing to know is that this creative power is bigger than your reason for using it. This means that your creative power is bigger than your problems.

Wonderful! Now what?

Next comes doing. If you don't follow what you know with constructive action, your knowing becomes stagnant. Lovely and inspiring maybe, but stagnant! What you know must move you into constructive action. Why not just start out with action and skip the knowing? Because action that follows knowing is intelligent action. It's not just doing for the sake of doing. Change that represents growth requires doing that represents intelligent action.

After a Sunday service some time ago, a man came up to me and said that he was more successful now in telephone sales than ever before.

"What's different now?" I asked him.

"Before I do anything, I take the time to know who I am," he told me.

In essence, by starting his day with knowing the truth about his own identity and accepting the inevitability of success, this man was linking intelligent knowing and constructive action in a way that was changing his life.

We are spiritual beings, living in a spiritual system, governed by our use of spiritual law. Taking control of the way we use spiritual law means taking control of the way we think. If we try to control people

and circumstances without first taking control of our own consciousness, we are bound to be disappointed. Unless we change our minds,
no permanent change can occur in our circumstances.

It's amazing how well people treat you when you know you are
centered in the Mind of God and then act as if this were so. It's also
amazing how circumstances become favorable when you know that
it's not what happens to you that counts; it's the way you react to
what happens to you. When you follow your knowing with a decision
to react in a healthy way, whatever is going on—whatever tack you
happen to sit on—becomes a circumstance you can deal with.

Every thought, every action is a creative act. You create your own
quality of life by the thoughts and actions you impress into the divine
principle of reality. Now that you know this, what must you do to create the life you want?

First, eliminate any thoughts that you are better than anyone else or
less than anyone else. You are neither. You are one with everyone at
a level that is changeless. Remember, people who need to think of
themselves as better are people who secretly believe they are less.

Second, eliminate any thoughts that neither build character nor
support your highest good. Replace them with thoughts that inspire
you to express your identity in God.

Third, accept the truth that you *can* think what you ought to be
thinking and keep from thinking what you ought not to be thinking.
Take control. Put your mind in gear and take yourself where you want
to go. Stop trying to impress people, and start impressing yourself
with the right ideas. Refuse to be petty, intolerant, or miserly.

Though you may want everyone to become aware of these great
truths so that they, too, can create the kind of life they desire, you cannot wait until they do. You must act on what you know, and you must
act now. You must live as if the only thing that has power to influence
you is your own thought. You must live the way you were designed to
live—understanding the divine principle and expressing its truth in
everything you do.

Living your life by these principles may make you an example to
others, but that's not the reason you are living by them. You are living
by these principles because you must act on what you know. Anything

less is unworthy of a human being that knows itself to be a spiritual being.

Whether you are confronting something as simple as sitting on a tack or something that seems much more complex, never forget that the creative power to change your life lives within your willingness to control your thoughts. Don't make the issue any more complex than this. Simply eliminate what doesn't belong and embrace what does. Take charge of your mind, and your life can become whatever you want it to be.

Get going! There's no time like right now.

DAVID J. WALKER is the founding minister of the Los Angeles Church of Religious Science and president of Religious Science International. Before studying for the ministry, he enjoyed a fifteen-year career as a professional singer. His weekly cable television show *Successful Living* airs on five local Los Angeles stations.

Creating or Miscreating

Joan M. Gattuso

Most people don't want to change.
They just want their toys fixed.
ANTHONY DE MELO

Life is about change. It is about lasting, permanent, total change that becomes transformation. It is about discarding the broken toys of life along with their broken modes of operation. More important than attracting "new toys," life is about learning how to create the desires of the heart.

To be successful at such creation, we must understand clearly the distinction between creating and miscreating. Every waking moment of our lives, we are engaged in one activity or the other. In our day-to-day, commonplace living, as well as in our extraordinary moments, we are sowing the seeds that will produce the crop of our future.

We sow and nurture the seeds that manifest as our lives' harvests through our conscious and unconscious thoughts, our feelings, our audible words, our inner-mind chatter, and our actions. These four, along with our desire and focus, are the primary components of creating and miscreating.

Creation occurs when we are awake, conscious, aware, and committed to our spiritual growth and our partnership with the divine. We create by using consciously the tremendous powers of mind that have been given to each of us.

We miscreate when we are ignorant of the power of mind we possess and the talents we have, or when we are aware of these powers and talents but do not engage them fully. We refuse to grow up and take responsibility for what we have been given in our lives. Instead, we take our tremendous power and direct it in unhealthy and harmful ways to produce heartache, hardship, and hurtful experiences.

When we act in such unskillful ways, we cannot rightly call the results we achieve *creations,* for true creation is the result of aligning our intentions, thoughts, feelings, focus, words, and actions with ultimate truth. Miscreations, on the other hand, are illusions we produce, the impermanent effects of misdirected energy. They are smoke-screen images, hallucinations, false manifestations of the ego, and though we often give them all our attention, they have no enduring reality. When we see our miscreations for what they are, they disappear.

The word *miscreation* became part of my thought and language a number of years ago when I clearly grasped its meaning in *A Course in Miracles:* "The fundamental conflict in this world then is between creation and miscreation." I came to understand that when we act out of fear or when we are addicted—whether to alcohol or to misery—we always miscreate.

In the past, like so many of us, I was very skilled at miscreating, though I called it creating. When something went wrong, I'd tell myself, "I certainly created a mess for myself this time," or "What a disaster was created for all those people." But messes and disasters are not creations. They're miscreations. When we can see miscreations for what they truly are—manifestations that are not firmly rooted in truth, more like a weed than a mighty oak—we are able to pull out the weeds and discard them. Until we reach this level of awareness, our sight is often so askew that we look at a weed and see it as an oak! Consequently, we feel powerless and live our lives as if we were.

When our thinking becomes distorted in this way, we often become incredibly skilled at playing the victim game, telling ourselves, "I'm really a good person. Awful things just keep happening to me, and I have nothing to do with any of them." Denying our power and responsibility for what is occurring in our lives does not mean that we are not powerful or responsible. It means only that we are unaware of our power. In fact, believing we are powerless is one of the primary ways we miscreate.

When we realize the incredible power of every thought, word, feeling, and action, we come to see that our miscreations are the inevitable end results of thinking, speaking, feeling, and acting in negative ways. Negative behaviors manifest as troublesome situations, unholy relationships, financial difficulties, debts, misunderstandings, and challenges of endless sorts.

Long ago, when I was unconscious in my personal relationships, I was highly skilled at miscreating. The ensuing results were unhealthy, unholy, painful relationships. It took years to extricate myself from their long-term effects and to accept that whenever we force, manipulate, or coerce another person or situation, we miscreate.

The principle that underlies such miscreations is the law of mind action. It tells us, "Thoughts held in mind produce after their kind." I have found this truth to be the bedrock on which we must build whatever good we desire in our lives. Just as acorns produce oak trees and ragweed seeds produce ragweed plants, so too our thoughts are seeds that produce full-grown results—beautiful and helpful creations and noxious and hurtful miscreations.

I have a friend, Marilyn, who argues that this law couldn't possibly be true in her life. She's a delicate-looking woman, sweet, kind, gracious, and polite, but burdened with an amazing capacity for negative thinking. One upset is followed by the next. Since something is bound to foil her plans, she is very hesitant about making any. It's always going to rain on her parade. As a result of her negative thinking, Marilyn's life is filled with struggle and brooding anger because her dreams have died.

Not long ago, her husband pulled me aside and asked in frustration, "Can't you do something with Marilyn? Her negativity is getting worse and worse. She complains constantly, argues with her grown children, and forever feels victimized by life. She's so damn sweet about what a victim she is, she's driving us all crazy!"

The truth of the matter is that for forty years, Marilyn has been sowing seeds of negativity, and as the law of mind action states, these seeds have been producing after their kind. The results Marilyn has been reaping are miscreations because they arise from falsehood rather than truth. Negative or false thinking, feeling, speaking, attitudes, and actions always show up as lack, sadness, struggle, heartache, disappointments, illnesses, lost opportunities, misunderstandings, and other negative manifestations.

Miscreations, I have come to understand, are the manifestations of a fear-based mind. In fact, they are the realization of any and all things that we have feared. We can help ourselves remember that miscreations arise out of fear by spelling *fear* this way:

> False
> Evidence
> Appearing
> Real

The phrase "false evidence appearing real" reminds us that the evidence that we are witnessing certainly looks valid, brimming with reality. But in fact, what we think we are seeing is an apparition—an illusory miscreation. Any situation that has arisen out of fear-thought or fear-filled emotion can only be a miscreation. When that same situation is seen in the light of true understanding, it disappears, because no matter how real a fear-filled situation may seem, it lacks a stable root structure. Pull up the shallow-rooted weed that is the outgrowth of fear-filled thinking, and it inevitably shrivels and dies.

Unlike fearful miscreations, creations are based on what can be called true reality. Everything that is spiritually and eternally true is subject to the same law of mind action, except that these thoughts, feelings, words, attitudes, and actions are grounded, not in negative thinking, but in spiritual law. Positive spiritual thoughts, feelings, words, attitudes, and actions show up as peace, joy, blessings, right outworkings, opportunities, health, success, well-being, fulfillment, satisfactions, happiness, and other positive and creative manifestations. What we truly create is founded upon the truth of our beings. What is based upon the spiritually true cannot help but be lasting and uplifting.

When we are awake, we use the power that God has given us in a conscious state of awareness. From this state of mind, we create what we truly desire and cease miscreating what we no longer desire. When we are engaged in miscreating, our lives are a soap opera, oozing with drama, chaos, and confusion. When we are engaged in creating, our lives radiate peace, serenity, and happiness. I've lived in both worlds, and believe me, the world of truth has it all over the soap opera world!

To use our energy consciously to create, we must direct it toward the positive, aligning our thoughts, feelings, words, and actions with our God-like qualities. Through such a shift in our perceptions, we meet our successes and still retain peace in our hearts. We become cocreators with God of a life of beauty.

JOAN M. GATTUSO, an ordained Unity minister, is founding minister of Unity of Greater Cleveland. She is also a best-selling author. Her books include *A Course in Love* and *A Course in Life,* and she has published numerous magazine articles. A longtime student of *A Course in Miracles* and a student of His Holiness the Dalai Lama, she has traveled widely to meet with world spiritual leaders. As a leader, teacher, and spiritual counselor, she introduces principles of transformation to those who attend her church and the classes she teaches.

I'll Do It Anyway

Jane Claypool

In 1965, I was thirty-three years old and had been widowed twice. I was so confused and shocked that I could barely attend to the lawyer's words. "We've found another $260,000 in the estate. You are a very wealthy woman."

"No," I answered. "Dick didn't have that kind of money. He didn't care much about money, and he spent what he had."

"These were Canadian stocks," the lawyer continued. "Ten thousand shares at twenty-six dollars a share. We're certain of the value."

"It's impossible," I replied. "I know what we had."

The lawyer cleared his throat. "My dear, sometimes husbands don't tell their wives everything about their financial investments. We checked the value of the stocks here and even called a Canadian broker. You'll never have to work again."

I left the lawyer's office believing what I had been told and a bit dismayed by the prospect of inheriting so much money. I was earning $10,000 a year as a schoolteacher, and my husband had been making a very nice income of $25,000 a year when he died. We spent our money on books, hobbies, travel, and education. Neither of us had much financial knowledge, although Dick had always dabbled in the stock market as a hobby. I had believed he usually lost money.

I knew the lawyer was a trained professional, so I had to trust what he had told me. He must know, even if what he said didn't fit anything I knew about my marriage.

During the next month I continued to teach school while I tried to figure out what I would do with the rest of my life. I could certainly continue teaching, but it seemed I should come up with a bigger dream, now that I had the means. I wanted to buy a house in the neighborhood where we'd been living and keep my daughter in the public school where she was happy. I had no social ambitions.

I was attending a Religious Science church at that time, and while I neither believed nor understood most of the messages I was hearing, I did learn some techniques for getting beyond other people's expectations and listening to my own inner voice. By the end of the month, I knew I wanted to quit teaching and become a writer. I had always loved books and stories, and now I had the opportunity to spend some time pursing that dream.

Almost to the day that I was truly clear about my dreams and plans—I would buy a house, take a summer trip, and become a writer—I received a letter from my lawyer. It was a final accounting of the estate. The ten thousand shares of Canadian stock were valued at twenty-six cents a share instead of twenty-six dollars! My inheritance had dwindled to about $2,600.

I realized that the stocks the lawyers had overvalued had been what Dick referred to as his "penny stocks." I was so pleased to erase any mystery about our marriage that I laughed out loud. Instead of being devastated, I was amused and relieved that our relationship was as trustworthy as I had always believed.

Then I remembered my dreams. I wanted a house, a trip to Europe, and a new career as a writer. In the last month, I had come to believe I could have those things. I had mentally claimed them. I had dared to dream, but now my dreams were in danger. I wasn't attached to the money, but I had come to count on the dreams.

Then in a flash, a new thought came to me. "I'll do it anyway," I said. Once I claimed the right to my dreams, I felt entitled to them, despite the new information. I used the money I got from Dick's life insurance to make a down payment on a house. I spent part of the estate on a ten-week trip to Europe for my daughter, my mother, and me. I used the rest to take a year off from teaching to take writing classes at the UCLA professional writer's program. Long before the money was gone, I had sold a novel and got some articles and poems published in magazines.

Though it was not as easy as I expected, my dreams did come true. Over the next thirty-five years, I published eighty books for teens, hundreds of articles in periodicals, wrote teaching materials and a column on real estate, and established myself as a successful writer. I now write metaphysical books and curricula and give workshops on writing.

My writing workshops include the five basic elements of my story:

1. Establish the vision.
2. Accept it completely in your mind.
3. Do whatever seems sensible to pursue your dream.
4. Be willing to refine the dream and to mold your activity to current conditions.
5. Be willing to take a risk.

It's uncanny how the steps for becoming a successful writer fit the formula we learn in New Thought for achieving success in any activity we choose.

The first step is having a true vision. Our motivation must come from within to be valid. It cannot be a goal we select because we think we ought to want it or because someone else thinks it would be good for us. All of our dreams and visions must come from the center of our spiritual wisdom in order to be real. My dream of being a writer was a deep calling.

Accepting the dream completely in your mind is the most difficult step for most people. I had a wonderful boost when I believed there would be all that money to smooth the way. Today I know there will always be the money to support a true calling because spiritual laws do support our deepest, most heartfelt dreams. As a Religious Scientist, I now know that the best way to accept your dream is to saturate your thinking with New Thought ideas. Reading books, meditating, and attending church services and workshops help. We learn that when we are accepting the dream as real, we are building what Religious Science founder Ernest Holmes called a "mental equivalent" and Thomas Troward called a "spiritual prototype."

It is important to pursue your dream in a way that seems sensible. Building contacts, sending out proposals, writing treatments, keeping a definite writing schedule, meeting deadlines, and learning to make an effective presentation are all important in building a career in writing. The same is true for most visions and dreams. If we want to be good parents, we must meet our children's needs one day at a time. When diapers need changing, we can't do it by building a spiritual prototype and quitting the field of action.

When you take appropriate action in the direction of your dreams, you are sending a message to the universe that you are serious. If you send out fifty resumes and the job comes from your uncle's brother-in-law, the resumes weren't wasted. The universe got the message and responded in a way you didn't expect. The response still came because of spiritual laws.

Refining your dreams to fit current circumstances also makes good sense. It is not giving up. Rather, it's finding another way to move forward. Let me give you an example. An inexperienced college graduate wants to be a sports writer, but the only position available at the newspaper is writing about local politics. When he takes the job, he is moving in the direction of his dream.

We need to pursue our dreams by taking short-term steps and keeping the long-term vision. If your dream is to have a million dollars by the time you are thirty, and on your thirtieth birthday you have half a million, don't collapse. Be grateful. Refine your thinking, and move forward. Never give up!

The last and most important of these steps is to take a risk. You must be willing to put your life where your dream is. I know people who have spent their lifetimes dreaming of being writers but never really put in the time to get anywhere. I know others who dream big dreams but don't send their work out because they hate being rejected. Yet rejection is a normal part of the writer's life. I also know writers who are stuck writing the same thing over and over because they are afraid to fail at something new. Their visionary flame gets old and tired and dies and all because they were unable to take a risk.

Since that day in 1965 when I said, "I'll do it anyway," I have followed many dreams and taken many risks. I now understand more, and I've devoted my life to writing and teaching about New Thought principles. Many people thought I was taking a risk when I made the space in my lucrative writing career to start a church, but I was my own authority. I knew I could count on spiritual laws to support my newer and deeper dream. I also knew that I am prosperous when I am living the life I have chosen. Success isn't really about money. It's about the ability to choose.

We are all built to evolve and change. We must dare to dream and dare to follow our dreams. If we are to be fully prosperous, we must be willing to "do it anyway," whatever the risk.

JANE CLAYPOOL is the founder of the Center for Positive Living, Carlsbad Religious Science Church in Carlsbad, California. She also serves on the board of directors of Religious Science International and as curriculum chair of its board of education. A prolific author, she has published more than eighty books for young adults under several names and has written feature stories and articles for *Writer's Digest*, *Catholic Digest*, the *Los Angeles Times*, and other publications. She is also author of the books *Wise Women Don't Worry*, *Wise Women Don't Sing the Blues*, and *Science of Mind Skills*.

Masters of Descent

Dr. Michael Beckwith

Who among us has not pondered the source of creativity, that divine force that expresses itself in humanitarian benevolence, works of painting and sculpture, music, poetry, literature, dance, drama, and sport? Demonstrations of excellence—a miraculous hoop shot, the human voice reaching a sublime note, a life dedicated to selflessly serving humanity—transport us to a realm of awe. A surge of life energy rushes through us, and we determine to discover and nurture our own creative powers. We are inspired to release those false inhibitions that sabotage our inner urge to self-express. So vital is self-expression to our self-actualization that psychologist Erich Fromm wrote, "I feel that the only thing that will save civilization . . . is a renaissance of the spirit—a rebirth of the belief in man himself, in his essential creativeness."

For many of us, the first step toward unlocking our cocreative destiny is a painful one. If we fail to grasp life's true purpose, we may suffer a spiritual identity crisis and spiral through painful experience after painful experience. Suffering, the great awakener, becomes our teacher.

But in the reflecting pool of harsh experiences, we begin to develop self-awareness—the first key to awakening to our role as cocreators.

However, "self-awareness without self-expression," wrote Dr. Ernest Holmes, "can almost as readily produce emotional disturbances as can the lack of self-awareness." So, as a second step in the process, we endure the frustration of being unable to express what we are starting to know. Then, miraculously, we realize that the creative urge pressing itself upon us has its origin in life itself. We begin to see that each of us is an intentional creation, an essential player on life's stage. Each of us is a cocreative agent, a partner with Spirit as it fulfills itself through the expression that is our individual life.

Our evolution toward our cocreative destiny now brings us to the question, "Why am I here?" We long to know our purpose, our soul assignment. This yearning is so intense that it may be considered a mandate from Spirit. It commands us to lay bare all denial of our true nature. It compels us to call forth our reason for being. We thirst to know life itself and to experience our place in it.

What a wonder, then, as our evolution continues, when we discover that the highest form of creative expression is simply this: "Be yourself." Each human life, we thrill to find, is the canvas upon which the soul paints the scenes of its unique pattern of unfoldment.

As the self-portrait emerges, a second question takes shape, "Who am I?" Our identity, we begin to see, is a partnership, an active and conscious cocreation with Spirit. This creative partnership demands that we be willing to break all agreements we have made with mediocrity. To tap into our originality, our purpose for being, we must stop staying small to please society, family, or friends, and be willing to accept the mantle of cocreative possibility.

The life choices we then make go far beyond settling on a career, or a life partner, or a means of creative self-expression. Rather, cocreative partnership with Spirit is nothing less than our agreeing to outpicture the unique face of God that we have come into being to express in all aspects of our existence. As we touch this knowing and open ourselves to it, the bonds of mediocrity shatter. We step into the realization that not only have we a right to be here, but we are essential to the completeness of creation. Knowing this, every action we take—every thought, word, and deed—becomes a piece of the unfolding creativity of the universe.

The implications of this way of understanding the purpose of human life are vast. There's no getting around it. As Spirit's cocreative partners, we must—all of us—become descended masters. As descended masters, we live under a mandate to be captured by Spirit's divine vision and to anchor that vision on earth through meaningful action. Our function in this life becomes twofold: We are to recognize who and what we are, and we are to cocreate that purpose with Spirit. A life lived to fulfill this goal takes discipline, a willingness to sit in the silence of meditation and prayer so that we can hear our reason for being whispered into the ear of intuition.

Not everyone is ready to take on the task of divine cocreation immediately. Many begin their evolutionary journey with a period—months, even years—of simple, task-oriented living. People at this level of evolution function like automatons. They wake up, eat breakfast, go to work, eat dinner, watch TV, procreate, sleep—just to begin the cycle all over again the next day! Yet, for many, a gnawing at the core of being causes them to question why they are not happy. These questions eventually move them from unconscious sleepwalking to the next stage of evolution, goal-oriented living.

Here people begin to set goals for themselves and to achieve them through willpower. Crossing completed goals off the list—the right job, the right investments, the right house, the right partner—is exhilarating at first, but in order to sustain this exhilaration, the to-do list must become longer and longer, more and more challenging. Sooner or later, these people discover that they will never arrive at true creative expression following this path. Frustration causes many to drop the masquerade of acquisition and accumulation and to adopt a truer form of purpose-oriented living, one that can be achieved only through spiritual means.

As these people wake up to Spirit, they'll often begin pushing a cart up and down the aisles of the spiritual supermarket, seeking the key to their divine destiny. Those lucky ones who discover the secret of disciplined spiritual practice touch their reason for gracing the planet. To be alive, they find, is to live a life full of love, beauty, and generosity, to give more than to receive.

From this point on the path, learning accelerates. Those who have begun to discover their destiny as cocreators step more and more fully into the expression of these divine qualities as breathed into the individual soul by the infinite. They may, from this point, continue to perform tasks in support of high-minded goals, but there is a significant difference: They act with nonattachment; their deeds become pure doing sprung from pure being. The canvas of life, they find, is much bigger, much broader than any individual human life. It is nothing less than the cosmos itself!

This discovery completes the process of evolution we were sent here to fulfill. Consciousness expands, and we are suffused with a sense of spiritual freedom and full-blown creativity. Life is changed forevermore, and we join the ranks of the masters of descent whose contributions to the spiritual evolution of our planet anchor heaven on earth.

When we drink from the well of inner creative energies, everything that outpictures as the details of our individual life becomes an expression of the divine creative process. Mundane activities—sweeping the street, cooking, washing dishes, changing diapers, mowing the lawn—turn into art forms. We become—each one of us—artists of living. Where we are, God is. Partnered with the spirit of life, each act allows more beauty to come into the world. When we become artists from this purview, everything that we touch, say, or do is a creative expression of our attunement with the divine inner muse. Even in sleep we create dream-life experiences.

You can tell a saint, St. Augustine once said, by the way that person picks up an object. Saints, like every other conscious artist of life, are so attuned with the Creator that they grace each thing they touch with ultimate respect as an act of divine love. Every movement becomes a creative act because it is imbued with connection to the actor's purpose on earth and vibrates with the oneness of all creation.

The Spirit within you is knocking at the door of your heart, reminding you that you are an exquisite, precious, and powerful being. Shine! Sing! Articulate what you are sensing, feeling, knowing! Be!

Now is the time for you to stand up within that immense power. Allow the tidal wave of the Spirit to flow within you and through you. That wondrous torrent of inspiration and creativity is everywhere present. It is yours for the asking right now! Make yourself available to it and consciously enter the sacred process of cocreation, because that which flows through you cannot flow through anyone else in quite the same way. Become a descended master of your own divine, radiant, creative expression.

May these words of one of our world's most creative spirits, Albert Einstein, light your way: "It can easily be seen that all the valuable achievements, material and spiritual, which we receive from society have been brought about in the course of countless generations by creative individuals. . . . Without creative personalities able to think and judge independently, the upward development is as unthinkable as the development of the individual personality without the nourishing soil of the community."

Part IV

Relationship

Introduction: Putting Love into Action

Rev. Mary Manin Morrissey

By the time my second oldest son, Rich, was twelve years old, I noticed that he was growing a little distant. Conversations occurred only when I sought him out, and my questions about school and friends were often met with grunts, nods, or blank stares. Whatever had happened to the little boy who loved to snuggle with Mom and share his every secret?

"Adolescence," I told myself knowingly.

Then I realized that Rich had been inching away from me for some time. Kids his age may test their independence, but Rich and I had always been so close. Now I thought about it and couldn't even remember the last time he'd so much as asked for my help with his homework. Rich had been seven years old when his sister was born and nearly ten when his younger brother came along. With the family growing, I wondered if perhaps he saw the place he occupied in it shrinking.

One night, I sat on the edge of his bed. Tucking him in, I said, "You know, Rich, I miss the connection that I've always had with you.

And no matter how many John hugs I get, no matter how many Jenny hugs I get, no matter how many Mathew hugs I get, there's a place in my heart where only you belong.

"Nobody else goes into that spot but you," I said. "I miss you when we don't connect."

My little adolescent is now a grown man with a child of his own. We celebrated his thirty-first birthday together over brunch. As we sampled each other's omelets, he suddenly asked, "Remember that night you sat on my bed and told me how I had a special place in your heart that was just for me?"

I nodded.

"That night changed my life," he said. "I knew then that I mattered as much as the other kids. Somehow, I thought that I mattered less. Not until you told me did I realize how much it meant for me to know I was loved just the same. I was as important as the others."

You are as important as the others. You matter. And while you may be unaware of the fact, you matter most of all to God. With so many people in the world, how can God possibly carve out time and space for every individual? Like Rich, you may distance yourself because you feel insignificant amid the masses. You may not even realize what a greater love means.

It's easy to acknowledge that all God's children are equally and divinely loved. But knowing that information intellectually and truly believing that you can have a powerful and personal relationship with your Creator are two very different things. How would it feel to awaken every morning knowing that you are not alone, that there exists a presence and a power that can guide you through your every waking hour? How might you behave differently if you accepted that there is a special place in God's heart that only you can fill? You may not know how much God values you. But once you begin to sense the degree to which you are divinely cherished, it changes your life.

In the following pages, we are going to read about relationships, the relationships we have with God, with ourselves, and with others. New Thought is a theology that advocates love in action. The people you will meet in these stories have transformed their lives by learning to love in a bigger way. By taking risks, venturing beyond their known borders, they have discovered that expressing love is the very purpose for which they were born, that the love they give out is but a small measure of the love their Creator has for them.

The New Testament promises that wherever we are, God is. But how often do we feel separate from any power greater than our own? I think sometimes that we mistake our own sense of isolation for an absence of God. Yet, God never leaves us. If we're feeling lonely, it's because we've moved away from God, not the other way around. God is present regardless of whether or not we acknowledge that presence. Parents, children, neighbors, and colleagues exist. We exist. We cannot make other people go away or escape ourselves any more than we can make God disappear.

So, we don't have a choice about whether or not we're going to be in relationships, but we do get to choose their quality and caliber. Relationships exist whether or not we desire them. How we choose to manifest them is up to us.

Loving relationships require diligent attention. Nothing in our lives will ever count for more, but so caught up do we become in the frenetic pace of everyday demands—the deadlines to meet, the schedules to keep, the errands to run—that relationships often get short shrift.

Every day, we have opportunities to put our love into action, by saying the words, offering the touch, demonstrating the feelings that turn ordinary relationships into something extraordinary. Do your loved ones know how much they matter to you? Sometimes we assume that our knowing is sufficient. But our knowing is not as important as their knowing.

We can make our interactions challenging, distant, and fraught with conflict so that loneliness pervades every moment. We can scratch the surface enough to get along and get by, without ever having a significant impact on another living being.

Or we can honor one of the fundamental principles of New Thought, which is: The Kingdom of Heaven is within us, and we are meant to realize this Kingdom on earth. This means that all the beauty and love and jubilation that we imagine to be reserved for the afterlife—all the joy we postpone for the future, or after our bills are settled, the kids are grown, or work has calmed down—can be experienced right now.

Everything we imagined as our reward for dutiful living, the payoff for all the pain and disappointment endured, doesn't have to be delayed until every detail of our lives is in order.

Look at the life of Jesus. Never once did he put off a miracle. Never once did he say, "You want to be healed? Let me get back to you on that." No, what he said to the infirm was, "Arise and be healed." The moment we actively connect with God, we harness the power that has been available to us all along.

We can have deeply rewarding, fulfilling relationships that make a visible difference in the lives of ourselves and others. We can awaken each morning and move through each day with the unshakable assurance that we are giving our utmost in love and being loved in return.

Regardless of our marital state, our current level of communication with our parents or children, we can bring love forward and fulfill our destiny as loving children of God. To do so requires that we live in a state of perpetual honesty, that we be willing to hold up a mirror so that we can see when we reflect love's presence and when we do not. We need to ask ourselves, "Am I missing any opportunities to express love?" "Am I offering love to those who are easy to love and withholding my caring from those who are not?"

The Kingdom of Heaven on earth is a club with open membership. No person is excluded from God's love, nor do we get to decide who is deserving of our compassion. Through practice, we gain the skill to find our way through the mire and maze of the times when we fail to put our love into action.

Through spiritual practice, we learn that love isn't something we reserve exclusively for a partner or our children, or something we withhold if those people are absent or if they disappoint us. Love isn't something we practice in our limited spare time. Love isn't something we can buy. And no matter how hard we try to hide, with God's help, love will always find us. We put love into action with words, deeds, and the knowledge that doing so is as much a part of our nature as breathing. The greatest works of Shakespeare are lovely to read, but the words don't truly resonate until actors breathe life into them upon a stage. Just as a play is written to be performed, love exists for us to demonstrate.

We are born to make a difference in the lives of those around us. There is no greater calling, no more lasting legacy. The people you will meet in the following pages have made their share of mistakes, but ultimately, they have found and are reveling in the Kingdom of Heaven on earth. Like most of us, they didn't always know how to tell others, "You matter to me." They didn't always know how much they mattered to God. But they do now.

I hope that they will inspire your own discovery.

A Short Course in Healing Relationships

Alan Cohen

One afternoon while house-sitting for some friends, I drove their new car to the beach. I turned the vehicle down a slim dirt road crowded with cars, hoping to find a parking spot. Soon I was greeted by a small red car heading in my direction. The driver leaned out and called to me, "Not even one space back there!"

"Thanks!" I called back and started to back out. Suddenly I heard a sharp *snap!* I looked to see that a protruding tree root had dislodged the rubber molding from the entire driver's side of the vehicle, leaving it hanging by a screw. I felt horrible. I tried to put the molding back in place, but it would not budge. Meanwhile the man in the red car waited patiently. "Just a moment!" I yelled.

After fussing with the molding for a few minutes, I realized I needed help. "Would you mind giving me a hand?" I asked him. The fellow walked over, and together we succeeded in popping the molding back into position. I thanked the man, he smiled, and I moved the vehicle for him to pass.

When I pondered the experience later, I realized that the point was not the bumper; it was the interaction. I was feeling frazzled and guilty, first for knocking off the molding, second for keeping this fellow waiting. He had a choice about how he could react. He could have been angry and impatient, or he could have been kind and helpful. He chose the latter path, and I felt released.

A Course in Miracles tells us that the only purpose for our relationships is to enjoy love. Because we are spiritual beings, the spirit of our activities either fulfills us or leaves us feeling empty. We may be tempted to believe that our lives are about doing things, manipulating stuff, and getting somewhere. In truth, our lives are about staying in our hearts and enjoying the adventure as we go.

Even so, we have hassles with people. We get upset, lose our tempers, blame others for our problems, and blame ourselves for theirs. We get caught up in appearances and forget our essence. So, what can we do?

First, we can forgive ourselves. Rather than using our mistakes to attack ourselves, we can use them to practice compassion and relief. Imagine that you are in a school called "relationship," and the curriculum includes making mistakes so you can learn. You are not expected to handle every situation perfectly. Observe little babies learning to walk. They fall down a lot. After falling for the sixth time, they do not throw their hands up in despair and exclaim, "That does it. I give up on walking!" They just keep trying. They laugh. They make a game of it. They keep going until they get it. And they do.

Next, we can give ourselves (and other people) the benefit of the doubt. We can choose a gentle, kind, or even humorous interpretation of any situation. While watching a video with my friends Patricia and Bill in their living room, I stepped into the kitchen to make some tea. Not finding a tea kettle, I took a Pyrex Mr. Coffee container and set it on the gas stove to boil some water. A few minutes later we smelled something burning in the kitchen and ran to see what it was. To my dismay, I found that the plastic handle of the pot was aflame. Quickly I blew it out, feeling embarrassed about starting a fire. To my surprise, Bill smiled and said, "Gosh, Alan, I didn't know you were such a good fireman!" What a lesson! I saw myself as an arsonist, and he saw me as a healer. The moral of the story? You can make anything out of anything.

We can also use difficult relationships to practice taking our power back. We feel pain in a relationship when we believe the other person has something we want or need, and we can get it only from them. We think they hold the key to the money, support, love, sex, power, wisdom, or security we seek. When they do not give us what we desire, we feel frustrated and angry. In such a situation we frame ourselves as empty, small, and less than the other person—a disservice to both of us.

If you have given your power away to someone, a good question to ask yourself is, "What do I think I need from him or her that I cannot get from myself?" This person is not the source of your good. He or she may be an avenue through which your blessings flow, but the river of abundance is not limited to any one person. Spirit is quite resourceful when it comes to delivering good!

I was invited by a well-known organization to speak at a large and prestigious conference. Feeling very honored, I looked forward to earning a large speaking fee, selling lots of books, and boosting my career. A week later I received a letter from the organization informing me that the person I had been hired to replace would be coming after all, and I was out. My heart sank. I felt disappointed and victimized. I stewed for a while, until a friend asked me, "Is there a gift in this for you?"

Suddenly I realized that my good was not dependent on this conference. There were plenty of other ways that prosperity could find me. Instantly my upset lifted, and I felt free. That lesson was far more valuable than any speaking engagement. Later the organization hired me for other events, and I ended up having it all—freedom *and* prosperity.

If you have experienced a conflict with someone, proactively hold a vision of love and harmony with that person. Love is still present. Affirm, "The God in me loves the God in you." Write or verbalize a list of all the things you appreciate about this person, and why you two got together in the first place. Then take a few minutes to visualize things working out in a way that leaves both of you feeling peaceful and satisfied. Ask yourself, what would be the best way this situation could work out?

After college I rented a house in the country with several other fellows. Soon we discovered that our neighbor, Mrs. Ryan, did not like us very much. We had several conflicts with Mrs. Ryan, and our relationship was strained. Then one night I went to a lecture on positive thinking, during which the teacher asked us to bring to mind someone with whom we were not getting along. Instantly Mrs. Ryan's face swam into view. Now, the teacher instructed, send the person love. This part was difficult. But I stayed with the exercise until I felt my heart open to Mrs. Ryan and could appreciate her.

The next day Mrs. Ryan approached one of my housemates and told him, "I would like to be friends with you. I know you are really nice fellows, and I think we can get along if we try." I was amazed! The only difference in our relationship was that I had sent this woman genuine love for a few moments. Spirit knows no limits of time or space, and the love we broadcast is received, felt, and has an immediate positive effect, often with observable results.

Finally, surrender your relationship to God. Ask your higher power to step in and accomplish for you what you have not been able to do. Let go of any demands, and allow love to lead the way. Once I was upset with a writer who had promised to interview me for a magazine. Months passed by, but she did not follow through. Then one day I went into meditation and released her. I decided that love and harmony were more important than the interview, and if Spirit wanted this conversation to happen, it would. If not, all was well. The moment I stood up from the meditation, the phone rang. It was the writer calling to make an appointment for the interview. The moment I released her, everything clicked into place.

Relationships offer us our greatest opportunities for awakening. Relationships can be hell, but with even a small investment of love, they can be heaven. As *A Course in Miracles* reminds us, "The holiest spot on earth is where an ancient hatred has become a present love."

ALAN COHEN is one of the most inspirational writers and speakers in the New Thought movement. He is author of the best-seller *The Dragon Doesn't Live Here Anymore* and *A Deep Breath of Life* and a contributing writer to the *Chicken Soup for the Soul* series. His syndicated column "From the Heart" appears in forty magazines. His interviews and articles have also appeared in *Science of Mind*, *Personal Transformation*, *New Woman*, *New Realities*, *Human Potential*, and *Visions* magazines. A sought-out lecturer and seminar leader, he is a frequent keynote speaker at national and international conferences. He resides in Maui, Hawaii, where he conducts retreats in visionary living. He also guides trips to sacred sites around the world.

United We Stand, Divided We Swim

Rev. Deborah Olive

I had rehearsed my answers in preparation for the interview. I knew that qualities such as competition, independence, and cleverness would be favorably received, especially if they were mixed with a healthy sense of humor. When asked to share my weaknesses, I would say that I tend to work too much. That, too, would be well received. The year was 1986, and I was two days away from an interview for a sales job with a Fortune 200 company. I knew "the drill," and I had every confidence that I would land the job. I did.

Today, I am a New Thought minister, and I have a broader perspective about people and the world we live in. I find that the values that are so well received in the business world are counterproductive to the challenges of our times. Life truly is easier, more interesting, and more fun when we honor and appreciate the gifts of those around us. When collaboration rather than competition is our first thought, we discover many effective and imaginative ways to cocreate our world.

Jack Boland, a Unity minister, has said, "Never let your good get in the way of your better." God calls us to give up the lesser, so we can claim the greater. What if we valued cooperation and collaboration more than independence and competition? What if we taught those values to our children? Most of the "teaching stories" from my childhood had a hero or heroine. Most also had a winner and a loser. Consider your background. Were you taught more about independence and competition or about cooperation and collaboration?

We live in complex times, when many of our challenges are system-wide and require the talents of many people. We must challenge the ways we have always done things. The era of the hero is waning, and an era that calls for cooperation and collaboration emerges more clearly every day. When we come to know that within each of us is a spark of divinity, a part that is so filled with potential we are absolutely equipped to meet the challenges of our times, we begin to see that our greatest contribution is not simply how we claim and express our divinity—what I call our "inner giant"—but how we might make giants of others. God is calling us to have soft eyes and an open heart—eyes that can see the unexpressed potential in others and a heart that is willing to encourage and cultivate others' unique gifts.

Bombarded by deadlines, expectations, and more data than we can process, it takes courage to make it a priority to connect with others and to value them for who they are. We live in a world that runs at a pace measured in nanoseconds, and we struggle to find the time simply to connect with our families and friends. At the same time, we realize that it is more important than ever to invest time and energy in connecting authentically with the "whole person." Such authentic connections help us to value others and to trust the potential that lies within each person. They help us know when it's appropriate for us to assume leadership and when we should step aside into a supportive role because someone else is better suited to lead. As our planet shrinks to village size, we must practice the art of blending our talents into a cohesive community, certain in the knowledge that God has given each of us a part to play in building a sustainable future.

Life is certainly willing to teach us the value of collaboration, but sometimes the cost of learning is frighteningly high. Fortunately, we don't always have to learn the hard way, through trial and error. Classes, workshops, books, spiritual communities, seminars, and corporate trainers have found ways to teach the value of collaboration in "laboratories for living." While there are no "quick fixes," such work can clarify and anchor our new understanding. When we enter into the process of learning the skill of collaboration, we find that we can learn much from other people's experiences. The following true story illustrates what I mean:

A group of oil company executives was midway through a week-long training adventure. The instructor called the executives together to provide instructions for the next task. The instructor filled a bucket with water from the river and pointed to the other supplies each team would receive. "Each team will get a half dozen two-by-fours, four inner tubes, a length of rope, and a bucket of water just like this one. You are to imagine that the bucket is filled with unrefined, high-quality oil. Your task is to build a raft with your materials that will support not only your bucket of 'oil,' but your entire team. You will then float from this beach to that large rock about five hundred feet down river. Remember, we like our river and do not want any oil spills. Not only does it anger the environmentalists, but it's harmful to the wildlife, and it's messy and expensive to clean up. Are there any questions? OK, then let's get started."

Three teams of six men formed. Upper and middle management filled two teams, and a group of engineers stayed together, forming a third team. A feeling of competition arose quickly as the teams discussed various ideas for accomplishing their task. Bragging that its strategy was best, each team began to construct a raft. It wasn't long before the first team was ready to launch. The raft floated about fifteen feet, out into the middle of the river, then it broke apart. Of course the team spilled its "oil," and everyone was soaked. Angry voices shattered the quiet serenity on the river. No one was spared a share of blame and accusations, and the task itself was declared "stupid." The team members lumbered out of the water, angry and wet.

Meanwhile, the second group, the engineers, finished their raft. It seemed quite "river-worthy" as it floated past the team that was just getting out of the river. Confident of their prowess and expertise, the engineers taunted the "wet team" with their laughter, remarking that they looked like drowned rats. The name-calling was soon replaced by self-congratulations. Team members patted one another on the backs and exclaimed how smart they were. When they pulled their raft out at the appointed spot and returned to the starting point, they were gloating.

The third team still had not gotten off the beach. The engineers' ridicule now extended to this team. "What are you waiting for, Christmas?" they jeered. Seeing the first team's failure and experiencing the humiliation heaped on them by the second team, the team on the beach began to argue. As tempers escalated, the conversation moved through blame to resignation. "What is the point of building this raft and floating some bucket of water down a river? What a stupid game! Why should we even do this?" Some members of the team took themselves out of "the game." They found a rock to sit on and folded their arms across their chests, determined not to participate. This team never got off the beach. The teams had now established their positions: a winner, a loser, and "not playing."

The game of "Don't Spill the Oil" certainly generated emotional fireworks. With the gloating, shouting, anger, and smugness escalating, the instructors knew the time had come to explore what was going on and to see whether some ahas could be realized. The planned discussion immediately turned into a free-for-all. The teams shouted at one another, and members of teams turned against one another, venting their anger and frustration. When the instructors restored order, each person was given a chance to share his experience and to tell what it felt like to be on his team. After more than an hour of sharing, feelings began to mellow. One question still lingered: "What was the point?"

Now it was the instructor's turn to ask a couple of well-timed questions:

1. Did anyone say this was a race?
2. Did anyone tell you not to help one another?
3. Would it have been more satisfying and enjoyable if everyone had won?

A voice of self-discovery rose from one of the men in top management as he realized the implications of this exercise to the company's last "real life" oil spill. "Oh, my!" he exclaimed. "Why am I so pro-grammed to compete instead of cooperate? Our response on that last oil spill took so long because we used valuable time finding someone to blame rather than responding to the call and working together to clean it up. We didn't even consider how we could help another team today. We had all the talent we needed to get all three of those rafts down the river, but we would have needed to work together. None of us can win unless everyone wins."

The instructor smiled and said, "Gentlemen, I think the world just got a little safer."

You and I also have the ability to make the world a safer place, in both small ways and large ones, when we collaborate rather than compete.

DEBORAH OLIVE is senior minister at Unity Center of Tacoma, Washington. Prior to attending seminary at Unity Village, Missouri, she was a sales representative in the medical field. With a degree in bio-chemistry, she artfully bridges the arenas of spirituality, science, and business. Her ministry is characterized by her integrity, humor, and commitment to spiritual transformation.

Taking Our Relationships
to a Quantum Level

Kathy Gottberg

Quantum physics may seem to be an unusual approach to talking about relationships. That is, until we understand that at the core of quantum physics, *everything* is relationships. Perhaps by opening up to the approach of new science, we can arrive at answers to questions about the quality, quantity, and depth of our relationships that have thus far eluded us.

To begin with, new science suggests that we view everything as a living system. While it may seem redundant to be admonished to think of ourselves as a "living system," in reality, we mostly think of ourselves as machines, distinct individuals made up of parts. When something goes "wrong" with us, we hire a mechanic—a doctor or some other expert—who can "fix" us. If some body part isn't working, we medicate it, repair it, or replace it. If our lives aren't working, we hire a therapist or counselor to do a "tune-up." We seldom think of ourselves as whole, interconnected, living systems. Even the concession that we are body, mind, and spirit seems to divide us into three parts.

We carry this same mechanistic model into our spiritual lives. The old scientific way of looking at things says that each of us, and the planet we inhabit, is a machine with parts to be analyzed, studied, and, if necessary, replaced. We were not taught that life is an interconnected whole. We were not taught that everything is in relationship with everything else. We were taught that if we take things apart, dissect them, we can discover their secrets. Even in metaphysics we are sometimes taught that God is a law to be figured out and then applied. Such thoughts reduce God to an absentee landlord or, worse yet, a clock maker. When we carry this mechanistic view to its conclusion, each of us, like everything else in the universe, is just a part of a ticking clock that is slowly winding itself down.

The old scientific paradigm held that once we discovered all the parts, the entire universe, and even God, would be understood. But about a hundred years ago, scientists searching for the smallest and most elusive parts of things made a huge discovery. They found that the elemental aspects of the universe were neither solidly one thing nor another. When things were reduced to their tiniest factors, they were not "one thing" at all. They were actually two! Sometimes the smallest factor was a particle, and sometimes it was a wave. Not a "wave thing" like an ocean wave, but a wave of possibility. In other words, the fundamental aspects of the universe are both particles and waves. You can imagine how distressing that discovery was to scientists who lived, as we all used to, in a comfortably predictable, either/or universe.

Science didn't like this new idea one bit. Unfortunately, the more physics researchers tried to disprove it, the more they proved its truth. No matter how they sliced them, the elements of the universe sometimes appeared as particles and sometimes as waves of possibility. Then, to add insult to injury, researchers discovered something else. They found that the person doing the testing, the observer, determined whether a factor appeared as a particle or as a wave. Horror of scientific horrors, they realized that there is no such thing as a completely objective point of view. Every person who observes something affects what he or she observes. We can try to pretend—and the old scientific model still hangs on tightly to this idea—that we can be impartial observers. But quantum physics proved that there is no such thing. What's even worse, experiments proved that the expectations of the observer seemed to "call forth" the result that he or she expected.

If every observer calls into being what he or she expects, even if only on the subatomic level, then the observer is bound into relationship with what is being observed. This simple fact explains the statement that quantum physics holds that everything is relationship. The stuff of the universe, all intelligence and matter, is made up of quantum elements that sometimes appear as waves and sometimes as particles. We observers go forth with our expectations, and in relationship with these particles, we "call forth" what we observe.

But the revelations of new science don't stop there. Consider for a moment that if humans are living systems and are always in relationship with the very stuff of the universe, then each relationship itself is a living system. What does this mean? For one thing, it means that any relationship is an uncontrollable, constantly changing dynamic that cannot be "fixed" because it's never "wrong." Up until now we've tended to think of relationships as "things." If a relationship is broken, we try to get it fixed. If we don't have one, we want to get one. If we lose one, we want to find one. We think of relationships just as we tend to think of ourselves, as separate, closed, and made up of parts.

Quantum theory suggests we are always in relationship. Now, our relationship may not exist in the way we want it. But any relationship is interactive, a dance between observer and observed. As the observer, we are constantly evoking or calling forth that which we observe. There's no escaping the obvious conclusion. We are ultimately responsible for the quality, quantity, and outpicturing of every relationship in our lives. Ouch!

How does this new understanding impact our day-to-day lives? How does it affect our relationships on the job, with our neighbors, with our children, and with our parents? How does it affect our intimate relationships, or our lack of them? For me, the most important conclusion is that the quality and the quantity of *all* our relationships are up to us. If we "call forth" from the stuff of the universe that which we see and experience, whether we have a relationship or not, whether our relationships are what we want them to be or something quite different, these conditions are merely what we have called forth. Like it or not, we are the cocreators of our relationships. If we don't like what we're getting, perhaps it's time to call forth, or expect, something new and different.

Probably the reason we don't embrace the new science approach to life, even though it has been around for decades, is because of the deep responsibility it demands. Quantum physics says that all of life is interconnected. If we were to embrace that concept truly, we would have to start taking care of one another, and our planet, in a completely new way. We'd also have to begin to acknowledge that if we are really cocreating our reality as we go along, we'd have to do the same with our relationships. Our relationships connect us with all human beings, the earth, and the universe itself, not just with one "significant other" who is here to fulfill our needs. The saying, "We're all One" becomes real in quantum physics. No longer can we say it's "me" against "them." From now on, it is always "us."

As seen through the lens of quantum physics, relationships are living, evolving connections that never "arrive" but are always "becoming." If we started judging the quality of our relationships in that light, we'd acknowledge that change, growth, and creativity are essential qualities of all healthy relationships. The new science approach may require us to be responsible for much of what we've ignored in the past. But the advantages of living in an evolving, creative hive of deep connection take us directly to an understanding of love itself. Love may just be that dance of observer and observed, that living system of which we and every other being and becoming thing is a dynamic participant. And isn't it love, after all, that we want from relationship in the first place?

I Don't Want Any God Stuff!

Rev. Sandra Lee Rudh

Charlie and Kate stepped into my office to discuss their upcoming wedding vows. Kate had asked me, as her pastor, to preside at their wedding, even though Charlie was not a churchgoer. Charlie was tall and thin with short blond hair, blue eyes, and glasses. Kate, a longtime church member, complemented him with her dark eyes and long dark hair. Both were in their early thirties.

Kate looked uncomfortable as Charlie began speaking. "I don't want a religious wedding or any God stuff," he said emphatically.

"I take it you don't believe in God?" I asked, smiling.

"Absolutely not," he replied.

Kate had prepared me for Charlie's resistance. My goal in speaking to him was to help Charlie achieve a level of comfort with a worldview that was basically spiritual, while still honoring his reason and his knowledge of science.

"I understand you are quite interested in science," I began. "How would you describe the nucleus of an atom? What goes on in the heart of matter?"

Charlie replied in scientific terms, using words like *pions, leptons,* and *quarks.* I attempted to sum up the content. "So, it seems that at the heart of matter, everything is just energy and motion. Would you agree?"

"Yes," Charlie said, and he began to smile as he realized I was asking questions for a purpose that he had not yet discovered.

"Would you say, Charlie," I continued, "that this world of energy and motion, atoms and molecules, seems to be well organized?"

"There's no doubt about that," Charlie replied. "From the microcosm of quantum physics to the macrocosm of cosmology, there is extraordinary and amazing order to everything."

"So, we could say that the heart of matter has energy, motion, and *intelligent design,*" I ventured.

"Yep!" he said with certainty.

Kate was grinning widely as she watched Charlie and me wind our way toward a unity of thought. Charlie was aware by now that I was gently leading him to some conclusions, and he was thoroughly enjoying the journey.

I continued our process. "I believe there is also a theory that states that the physical world emerges from one holistic field, in which all information is known everywhere at the same time—a field wherein all possibilities exist."

Charlie was laughing. "I can see you have been doing your homework, Reverend. That sounds like David Bohm's implicate order."

"Yes! And material reality comes out of that order and enfolds back into that order, with each part of physicality having an imprint of the whole."

I was ready now for the final point. "So, let's recap. Our physical world of energy, motion, and information emerges from a nonphysical realm of all possibility, where all information is known everywhere."

Charlie nodded in agreement.

"OK, Charlie," I said, "here's one last point to consider. Quantum physics tells us that the physical world is not as real as it appears. In fact, the smallest particles of matter seem to exist in a nonphysical state called a 'probability wave' waiting to become part of the physical world. As I understand it, these particles remain in a probability wave state until they are observed by a human mind, at which time they appear as tiny pieces of matter with a particular location."

Charlie and Kate were both laughing. "I think this is a setup, Rev!" said Charlie. "Don't you?"

"I confess!" I said with a smile. "I have been reading my science books. But, I don't think the word 'observe' is complete enough," I continued. "I believe we must observe with our physical eyesight and become *aware* of what we are observing. I prefer to use the word 'awareness.' As we become aware of something in our thinking mind, we affect its emergence into physical reality."

"So," Charlie said, "where is this leading?"

I had been working toward this moment. "I would like to call the one holistic field of all possibilities by the name *God*. God is that from which everything is made."

Charlie's face was relaxed and his eyes were bright as he spoke. "I never thought of it that way. It's a really different concept, but it makes sense."

I continued. "The world we live in is not really solid at all, but just energy, information, and motion. It is therefore quite changeable. Human thinking and awareness create an action upon this field. Or, to put it another way, human thinking creates a connection with God. That action creates our physical world. In other words, thinking makes it so. And here is the best part, Charlie. If we change our thinking, we can actually change our reality! We could, if we choose, call this mind action an *affirmative prayer*."

Charlie said nothing. He simply took Kate's hand and smiled.

"One last thing," I said. "Since the holistic field, or implicate order as you called it, is a unified field with all information known at every part, and since we human beings have emerged out of that field, then all knowledge and all possibilities are available to us."

"What are you going to call that?" Charlie teased.

"I call it *unconditional love*."

Charlie looked at Kate with loving eyes. "I guess we can have a religious ceremony after all," he said. "But can I ask one thing, please?"

"What?" I wondered.

"Could you just leave out the word *God?*"

"No problem, Charlie. No problem at all!"

SANDRA LEE RUDH is pastor of Spiritual Growth Center, Eugene Church of Religious Science, Eugene, Oregon. She was founding minister of Mt. Shasta Center for Positive Living. Her articles and daily treatments have appeared in *Science of Mind* and *Creative Thought* magazines. She is also author of *Religious Science Society: Starting from Scratch* and *Growing,* an illustrated booklet of aphorisms and stories. She gives lectures and seminars on New Thought topics in California, Oregon, and Washington.

Healing Our Relationship with Church

Rev. Dr. Toni La Motta

A number of years ago, I was quite involved in both taking and giving Ira Progoff's Intensive Journal workshops. In one exercise in these workshops, participants are asked to list the organizations and institutions that have been or still are part of their lives. Doing so helps people to be conscious of the groups to which they belong—social, political, economic, ethnic, and religious. When I first did this exercise, I listed the fact that I am a woman, an Italian, and a New Yorker by birth. I also listed the Catholic Church, since I had spent over thirty years in the Church and had been a member of a religious community for sixteen of those years.

Once you've made your list, you choose one group to work with during the exercise—the one that calls most loudly. Up until that moment, I hadn't realized that I had a lot of unfinished business, not only with the religious community I had been part of but also with the Catholic Church itself. Clearly, it was time to work on healing my relationship with church.

In the exercise, we first listed the ten or so major events that marked our relationship with the institution or group. As I listed these, I began to realize that my identity was quite bound up with being Catholic. (I was still in the church at that time.) We then personified the institution and began a dialogue, writing first as ourselves and then letting our subconscious reply in the name of the institution. I found myself pouring out resentments, sadness, and anger, discovering as I did so that some of the beliefs I had swallowed as a practicing member of the church were keeping me from moving forward with my life. I found that I was struggling particularly with my role as a woman in a male-dominated world, a position that church hierarchy and doctrine perpetuates. I also realized that the vow I had made when I entered my religious community to live in poverty was still guiding my life, though it had been years since I had left the community.

After writing for some time, along with these "negatives," I eventually got in touch with some wonderful memories and with a deep sense of gratitude. I came to realize that it was through the church that I began a meditation practice and cultivated a mystical understanding of life. I also had the privilege of knowing personally some exceptional thinkers and extraordinary human beings and had been exposed to teachings and experiences that transcended anything I could have found elsewhere. Though I later left the Catholic Church, I began that day what has become my life mission—to heal my own and others' relationships with God and religion, but particularly with church.

Because I have made this commitment, I often draw to me people who have issues with the whole idea of church, or with specific church-related incidents from their past. As a minister, I meet many people—even other ministers—who have an adversarial relationship with the whole idea of church. Some are quite aware of their negative feelings and openly avoid even using the word "church." Others seem to be unaware of how their negativity is blocking their ability to experience more good in their lives. Every unhealed relationship affects every other relationship we try to have. Until we heal the painful relationships of the past, we can never fully experience a loving relationship in the present. This truth applies to relationships with individuals as well as those with institutions like the church.

Say you're ready to undertake the task of healing your relationship with church. Where should you begin?

Perhaps the first step is to write or tell the story of your relationship. One of my students recently wrote me about hers: "I am one of the victims of a 1950s–1960s church upbringing. I have been through a lot of experiences with religion—none of them positive. I have a terrible emptiness these days as a result of the loss of my faith. It brings daily confusion and sadness. I have so much antagonism toward the church—all church(es), and I have yet to find peace with my anger. It's a long involved story, but I can tell you that the church left me feeling personally responsible for all the ills of the world!"

I invited my student, as I invite each of you reading this who share a similar antipathy to church, to spend some time being grateful that you have been able to acknowledge a major life block. Being aware of your negative feelings gives you a basis for working to heal them.

Also congratulate yourself on being ready to begin a process of healing. Know that you are undertaking this work not only for yourself but for all of humankind. Every act that reminds us that we are not separate individuals but one humanity facing a common challenge brings us closer to the actual experience of being one. Know that healing your relationship with church is sacred work. Invite yourself to be gentle.

The first stage in any healing is to acknowledge any sense of victimhood. Allow yourself to remember any experiences with church or church teachers and leaders that made you feel as if someone or something out there was trying to "get you" or was causing you to do something you did not choose. Feeling that you're out of control, that something or someone is making you do something, can be quite demeaning. In the case of church, many of us have suffered through childish or victim relationships with church rules or authority figures. Though we may have felt that "we were just doing what we were told," the loss of personal control can manifest as resentment and anger.

If this is true for you, allow yourself to acknowledge any anger, rebellion, or resentment that you may have felt. Ask yourself whether these feelings persist in the present. Now, gently remind yourself that these feelings are holding you back from a full spiritual life and that you want to be free from them. Find someone you can trust to whom you can tell your story. Alternately, write in your journal about your particular experiences, as my student did. Get it all out on paper. Allow yourself to acknowledge the pain, the anger, and the rejections.

Next, you might write a dialogue between yourself and your church as I did in the Progoff workshop. Alternately, you might write a letter to your particular church denomination as a whole. Put into words all the things that upset you. Give yourself permission to vent completely the feelings you might have. Go ahead and allow yourself to relive the feeling of victimhood you may feel deep inside, even though your adult consciousness knows that everything in life is a choice and that there are no real victims.

You may be surprised at what you find when you write. If you hang in with the process of discovery long enough, you may uncover, as I did, some sense of gratitude buried beneath your anger. I see this happen again and again with people I counsel.

Finally, acknowledge that church, like all human institutions, is imperfect, but that the function it serves, bringing you closer to God, is a sacred task. Promise yourself that you will not allow any negative experiences you may have had in the past to get in the way of a full and rich spiritual life. Pray for help in healing the hurts of the past. Pray for a new mind and new heart open and ready to receive the gifts that religion and church can bring—a vital relationship with the One Life that is God.

TONI LA MOTTA is pastor of Church of Religious Unity in Alpine, California. Formerly, she was president and owner of Technical Learning Institutes, a software training company serving Fortune 500 companies. She has given motivational and inspirational lectures and training seminars specializing in recognition and management of change. She has also taught college-level courses in business leadership, quality, and communications and has worked as a marketing director and as a programmer and systems analyst. She is author of the book *Recognition: The Quality Way* as well as many articles in technical anthologies and journals. She is a frequent keynote speaker at business conferences.

Undying Gratitude

Rev. Petra Weldes

Thursday. My dad died today.

"He could go in the next twenty-four to forty-eight hours," the doctor said when I arrived at the hospital on Saturday. That was a big surprise. I'd been told only last week that the cancer had returned and that it was terminal. I thought I was coming to help his wife settle him into long-term nursing care with hospice waiting in the wings. But there he lay, in ICU. "All we can do now is make him comfortable," the doctor said.

On Sunday evening Dad was moved to a private room, and his wife and I began our vigil. Standing by the bed I told my Dad how much I loved him. I named all the people who had sent their love to him. I assured him we were all taking care of one another, especially his wife. He had been so worried about what would happen to her. Maybe he was completely unconscious from the morphine drip, but I felt that his spirit could hear me. His wife told him to relax and rest easy now, for we were here with him.

When we returned to the hospital on Monday, we didn't really know what to do. I wasn't going to just sit there watching and waiting and wondering whether each breath would be Dad's last. What were we doing here anyway? What was the purpose of sitting by his bed, for surely, after all the years of pain and suffering, dying would be a grateful release into freedom and peace?

I felt our purpose here was simply to fill the room with a loving presence, to let Dad know that he was not alone and that he was surrounded by love, and to remind him that as we were lovingly releasing his spirit on this end, someone was waiting with loving and open arms to greet him on the other side. "Be at peace, Dad. There's nothing to fear. We are here who love you. Follow the light to the love waiting on the other side."

Whenever I was alone with Dad, I felt an inner urging to sing and pray his spirit home. I found myself reciting the Lord's Prayer or the Twenty-third Psalm. Often I sang to him.

We'd discovered a little meditation room in the hospital and took turns every day going down there and praying for release and peace. The nurses were compassionate, but it felt like living in the twilight zone. Would this never end?

Tuesday evening I felt so strongly about not leaving Dad alone that I requested permission to spend the night. The nurses brought in a little chair that folded into a bed and made me a place. Lying down around midnight, I could hear the sound of my Dad's breathing and wondered if this was the "death rattle." How was I ever going to sleep with that? Wouldn't it be too weird and spooky?

As I lay there next to him, I found the room was bathed in peace. I sang a hymn I'd learned in church many years before. The words seemed appropriate to help sing his spirit home:

> Into the Presence would I enter now,
> For I am surrounded by the Love of God.
> Let me be still and listen to the truth;
> Let every voice but God's be still in me.
> Let me remember
> I am one with God;
> Peace to all persons who are one with me.

Let me remember what my purpose is;
My will step back and let love lead the way.

About 1:30 or 2:00 A.M. I felt my dad's presence leave the room. It was very peaceful. At 3:30 or so the nurse came in to check him. His breathing and blood pressure had slowed so much, we both thought, "This is it." I wrapped us both in love and peace and, surprisingly enough, fell asleep.

"What are you still doing here? Don't you know you're not supposed to be here anymore?" his wife asked Thursday morning as we entered the hospital room for one more day. We'd pretty much said everything we felt we needed to say days ago, so we were filling the time and the room with our voices and presence by playing endless games of canasta. It felt fitting somehow. I'd grown up playing all kinds of games, and my Dad and his wife had loved playing canasta in the evenings. The game gave us something to focus on, but mostly it filled the room with something we had all really loved doing together. "OK Dad, you'd better help me here; she's beating me again!"

I'd awoken that morning knowing today was the day. Agitated and antsy all morning, I went to the meditation room to try to settle myself and to pray for my dad's release. Not once had my dad realized that I had come from Texas to be with him. I knew he was gone; just this cloak he'd worn for years lay in the bed, and he didn't seem quite able to let go.

As I sat in the stillness and prayer, a deep, unfathomable feeling of gratitude overwhelmed me. Such thankfulness flooded my being that I could almost not contain it. Gratitude to be here to ease the time for both my dad and his wife. Gratitude for the loving family, home, and church I had to go home to. Gratitude for all the times my dad and I had walked in the sun looking for wild flowers. Gratitude that I'd been able to forgive him for the anger, alcoholism, and abuse of my childhood. Gratitude that my spiritual practice had taught me how to heal my relationship with him despite his continued alcoholism and that I had learned to accept that his conditional love was the only love he knew how to give. Gratitude for all the things he had taught me, especially about business. Gratitude for the gifts he'd given me and all the times he'd helped me when I needed it. Gratitude that in some measure my faith had sustained him at times when we'd talk and that our church had become a second home to him.

With enormous peace I returned to the room. At 4:12 P.M. we realized that his gasping breathing had suddenly changed and became very quiet. As one we stood up and moved to the side of the bed. Touching his head and his arms, we whispered our love and our faith. At 4:15 he released his last breath, and I said through my tears, "Goodbye, Dad. Thanks for everything!"

Thursday. My dad died today. His breath has been released from the restless tides of this life, and he is dancing in the sun with the Living Presence of Life. In gratitude, I grieve and rejoice!

PETRA WELDES is senior minister of First Church of Religious Science in Dallas, Texas. She was founding and senior minister of Renton Church of Religious Science in Renton, Washington, and served on the faculty of the Ernest Holmes College in Seattle, Washington. Her special area of interest is the United Church of Religious Science youth movement. She served as chair of the UCRS Youth and Family Ministries Committee and wrote its teen curriculum. She consults on organizational development and leads board retreats for Religious Science churches, and she facilitates spiritual, meditation, and ministerial student retreats.

Nobody Has to Lose

Rev. Jerome Stefaniak and Stavroula Stefaniak,
LMSW-ACP, LCDC, LMFT

Have you ever spent endless hours trying to convince your partner that your point of view or what you want is the right thing for both of you? Have you ever given in to your partner just to keep the peace, only to find yourself feeling resentful? These scenarios are very typical variations of what happens in relationships when we get stuck in our need for power and control and believe that only one person can win an argument. In a conscious, healthy relationship, on the other hand, it is possible to reach a win-win solution to every conflict. No one has to lose in order for the other person to prevail. This highest stage in a relationship is called *synergy*.

What is synergy? Synergy is an experience in which the combined result is greater and more satisfying than what you'd get if you simply added together each partner's individual contribution. One plus one generally equals two, but when synergy is involved, there is a greater pooling of inner resources, and one plus one equals something more, and more wonderful, than two! That is because in a synergistic relationship, the partners know that there is a larger presence in their lives.

They realize that their relationship is not dependent solely on their individual bits of knowledge but on a greater knowing that there is always an answer to any conflict and that all they need do is share their truths, open their hearts, and let their divine selves lend a hand. When they do, the "win-win" concept begins to bloom.

To reach synergy, it is imperative that we open up to the wisdom that is within each of us. It is also imperative that we open up to the wisdom of God, which may be the same thing. When my wife, Stav, and I have a disagreement, we no longer try to solve it ourselves—OK! We do try to solve it ourselves, for a while. But when we finally get calm and centered, we offer the problem up to God. We tell ourselves that there is no problem so big that God in us cannot solve. We tell ourselves and each other that there is an answer that will make both of us happy, that there is a highest thought that will support the growth and happiness of both of us. We tell ourselves and each other that we want a win-win solution, that is, Stav can win and feel good about the outcome, and I can win and feel good about the outcome.

Just stating the fact that there is an answer that will satisfy both sides starts the process of healing, because it concentrates the power of our minds toward formulating an answer, as opposed to wasting that power trying to convince each other about who's right and who's wrong. Surrendering the problem to God allows our minds to be open to new ideas and possibilities. The answer may come in a day, a week, or a month. Stav and I have learned to relax and trust that God will always help us find a solution, and that any solution that God provides will always make both of us feel as if we have won.

Remember that we create our world through our thoughts. If you believe that a certain conflict is unresolvable, what do you think you create by the very power of your thoughts? An unresolvable conflict! In such cases, it is your own thoughts that keep you trapped. When you change your thoughts about an argument, when you both agree that there is an answer and that you will find it, with God's help, you have channeled the power of your minds toward finding the answer.

You need to know, though, that when you commit to finding an answer that will work for both of you, each of you may end up changing your mind about what you originally wanted, but the ultimate answer will be one that both of you will still feel good about. As you move toward synergy, it may even initially seem like you are going backward. That is because as a couple works out a problem, they tend to experience every stage through which a typical relationship evolves. Those stages are Individuality, Competition, Compromise, Cooperation, and Synergy. Let me give you an example of how this process works.

Several years ago, Stav and I were planning a three-week vacation and couldn't agree on where to go. I wanted to go to Seattle, to introduce Stav to my friends, the mountains, and the islands. Stav wanted to lie on a sunny beach (*Individuality*). We began to argue the merits of each position, trying to convince the other that we had the better plan (*Competition*). So we went to a travel agent to see what was available and to book a flight. During the discussion with the agent, it seemed as if Seattle would be the cheapest and easiest, and so, even though Stav didn't totally agree, we booked a flight to Seattle (*Compromise*).

Luckily, we had an alert travel agent who perceived that we were really not at ease with our decision, and so she told us that she would reserve our seats but would not write the ticket until the next morning to give us time to think about it. We agreed and left for a dinner engagement with a friend who had just flown in from San Diego.

On the way to dinner, we decided that neither of us felt good about the outcome. I felt guilty for getting my way, and Stav felt disappointed and somewhat resentful because she still wanted to go to the beach. And so we decided to release the trip as it was and see if there was a higher plan. We offered our vacation to God and asked him to help us.

As we drove, Stav shared her feelings. "Jerry, this has been such a hard year for us. I just want to relax. I need to be in the sun and be pampered. We've worked so hard, and we need this rest. It doesn't have to be the whole trip, but I do want us to spend some time on the beach. What is it you really want?"

"What I really want is mountains. It's been years since I've seen snow-covered mountains, glaciers, and valleys, and I miss them. That is what's important to me. The friends in Seattle we can see anytime, but right now my soul yearns to be in the mountains. And it doesn't have to be the whole trip either, but I do want some time in the mountains."

Just then I had a thought. "You know," I said, "our friends Jay and Sandra live in Colorado. What would happen if we drove up there and stayed with them? We can visit the mountains for a week or so and then drive back to Texas and spend the rest of the time at the beach on Padre Island, on the Gulf Coast."

Stav thought about this new plan and agreed. It felt like we had found the way to have our mountains and our beach (*Cooperation*). But there was more to come.

Later, while having dinner with our friend Robin, we told him about our vacation decision, and he piped up. "You know, guys, I'm going to be out of town during that period. If you want, you can fly into San Diego from Colorado instead of driving back to Texas and stay at my apartment and use my car. I live only a few blocks from the beach."

And so we altered our plans. We drove to Colorado, we had a nice visit with our friends, and I got to see my snow-covered mountains and elk. For a few days we rented a little cottage by a rushing stream and watched droves of hummingbirds as they fed at the feeders. I love hummingbirds, and I didn't realize that they were so prolific that time of year. It was an unexpected bonus for me. We both felt refreshed and rejuvenated and enjoyed the mountains immensely. Then we flew from Colorado to San Diego and spent another ten days in the sun. We also went to Disneyland, which was a dream Stav had had for years. It was an unexpected bonus for Stav.

The outcome of the trip was due to *Synergy*. Not only did we get what we both wanted, but we got more! And with greater ease!

There is no problem that can stand up to the combined will of two people and God. Arguments about money, bills, sex, kids, or food stand no chance when addressed honestly and responsibly with a determination to find a win-win solution. Make a new agreement with yourself right now. Commit to always finding the answer in which nobody ever has to lose again. You'll be happier, and so will the world.

JEROME STEFANIAK has been a spiritual teacher and breath integration practitioner for twelve years. With his wife, Stavroula Stefaniak, a licensed psychotherapist, he teaches workshops on prosperity, relationships, anger, self-esteem, and sexuality. He also teaches classes in *A*

Course in Miracles at Unity Church of Christianity in Houston, Texas. He is the author of *Compassionate Living: Everyday Spirituality* and *Intimacy in Action: Relationships That Feed the Soul.*

STAV STEFANIAK is a state-licensed psychotherapist and breath integration practitioner in private practice, with more than twenty years of experience in the mental health field. In addition to her individual, marriage, and group counseling, she presents workshops, helps develop community programs, and speaks at national conventions. As a spiritual psychotherapist, her goal is helping people transform their lives whether they are dealing with health, relationship, or personal issues.

The Key to a Life More Abundant

John Randolph Price

Understood in its fullness, the word "relationship" reminds us that we are connected to all that exists throughout this universe and beyond. This connection, which extends through both the physical and spiritual realms, operates through the law of cause and effect. Whatever we think, say, and do is recorded in our personal energy field. It also goes forth in time and space to produce a corresponding reaction that, sooner or later, boomerangs back to us. We experience this reaction most profoundly in our dealings with people, beginning with the inner circle of our families and radiating out to include friends, neighbors, acquaintances, associates in the workplace, and even strangers.

As Paul put it, "Whatsoever a man soweth, that shall he also reap." That's the principle here. Once we understand it, a whole new world opens up for us, and we see how important it is to send out only vibrations of harmlessness.

How do we sow correctly? Much has been written about loving unconditionally, but in the human scheme of things, that's easier said than done. In fact, there are times when loving a particular person seems like a mission impossible. I've felt that way, and perhaps my experience can help you open your heart when it seems as if you've lost the key to a life more abundant.

My family and I live out in the country on several acres in a serene and beautifully wooded area. One day our new neighbor began bulldozing his property. None of my business, right? Maybe so, but when he mowed down hundreds of large oak and cedar trees—literally scraped the land, leaving nothing but rocks, dirt, and weeds—I felt that my lovely environment had been brutally attacked. He and his wife just didn't like trees, they said; they blocked the view of the rolling hills.

As I watched the massacre and heard the cracking and crashing, I froze in place. I was probably in a state of shock. After a time, my daughter came out of the house and tried to persuade me to turn away from the debacle. She said I was acting as though I was watching a horrible accident with morbid fascination. She was right, but this was no accident. In the days to come, I didn't feel much love for that family next door. I walked the fence line, staring at the denuded land and the burning logs with angry eyes and gritted teeth.

Finally I realized that I wasn't helping myself or bringing back the trees with that kind of attitude. I had been working on a new book. Now I had writer's block, and I was feeling physically congested and generally out of sorts with everyone. It was clearly past time for me to change my mind and get back on the happiness train, my usual conveyance for moving through life. After all, the neighbor hadn't really done anything to me. It was my reaction to what he had done that was causing the problem.

The first thing to do? Forgiveness, of course. To begin with, I had to forgive my own thoughts and emotions. I really didn't want to hang the guy by his toes from the top of a tree while I berated him with offensive words. (I have a very vivid imagination.) Through contemplative meditation, I was finally able to forgive myself for thinking and feeling in such an angry way.

Now my attention turned to the neighbor. To forgive means to give up all resentment. Oh boy, that was tough! Then my wife, Jan, said, "We can forgive them for not being the way we want them to be—

lovers of trees. Let's do that now." We went into the silence with that thought, and after a time, I felt my indignation release. Forgiving them for not being the kind of neighbors we wanted them to be was a plain and simple way to turn off the fire from under the emotional boil. And when that was done, the door to love opened a crack.

But unconditional love doesn't begin with focusing outward, trying to love someone else when, on some level of consciousness, we don't feel they really deserve it. That process is devoid of healing and doesn't yield a lasting result, because after a time, the linkup of mind and emotions shifts, and the door to love closes. No, the initial outpouring of love must flow to ourselves, to our divine nature, to the Lord Self within that represents our true identities. That's what the Bible means when we are told to "love the Lord your God with all your heart, and with all your soul, and with all your mind." That Lord is not something separate and apart from us. It's the very Spirit of God, our divine consciousness that constitutes the only reality of our beings. As we gaze on this indwelling master self, what is there not to love?

Through this love affair with our holiness, we are lifted to a higher frequency in consciousness. Only then are we able to fulfill the other part of the commandment: "You shall love your neighbor as yourself." I proved to myself that this order of doing things is the right one, for as I took on the master love vibration, I was finally able to love those neighbors, with no strings attached. I prayed for them, too, although I recognized that whatever consequences they might experience as a result of their actions—such as the absence of birds and squirrels, or an overheated house in the summer without the shade trees—would be an educative experience for them. Nothing bad—simply a lesson in the law of cause and effect, just as I had learned.

Let us never forget that we are always, day in and day out, "involved in relationships." Being related to everyone in our world is the connecting link between heaven and earth. It is truly the key to a life more abundant.

As an analogy, think of a fine automobile—top of the line, luxury throughout, with a high-performance engine, superb transmission, and a fail-safe electrical system. Put your consciousness into that vehicle, and for a moment, think of it as yourself. Come on, play the game with me! Experiencing your oneness with the car, you might say "it's heavenly," but then consider, what's between you and the earth? Four round things called tires. And while you may be the most technologically advanced automobile in the world, able to accelerate with breathtaking speed, you're not going anywhere if one of those tires goes flat.

In this analogy, the tires represent our relationships, the connecting link that allows us to roll through life with joy. Being four in number, the tires correspond to the spiritual, mental, emotional, and physical aspects of our being. If we're not connecting with people on the spiritual level—understanding the unity of all life—we've got a flat. If we're not mentally in tune with people—knowing the truth of each person's divine identity—we're in a deflated state. The same thing is true on the emotional and physical levels. If we're hypersensitive in our feeling nature or agitated physically, we're negatively grounded and immobilized. When that happens, the energy is blocked, and the power to do, be, and have is impeded. Then suddenly, or over time, we begin to experience financial problems, physical ailments, or a sense of failure in our work. In essence, through our generating of negative forces in our relationships, we have disturbed the equilibrium of the universe, which at once begins to correct itself to bring things back into balance—beginning at the point of the disturbance.

Again, this reaction is nothing more than the law of cause and effect in action. No one ever does anything to us; we do it to ourselves. Our lives are never controlled by other people, events, or circumstances. Once we understand this principle—that whatever we give out we're going to get back—we can begin working with the law instead of against it. Then, through the harmonizing of all relationships, our world reflects back to us the natural order of life: abundant prosperity, radiant health, creative success, and a continuing love-one-another attitude that makes it all possible.

This is a benevolent universe, and all that is good, true, and beautiful is ours now. Isn't it time to accept our good and enjoy a life filled with love and peace? We can when we untangle the knots in our relationships.

I think I'll go call my neighbor and invite him over for a glass of wine. Maybe I can talk him into converting his land into a vineyard.

JOHN RANDOLPH PRICE is an internationally known lecturer, best-selling author, and cofounder and chairman of the board of The Quartus Foundation for Spiritual Research, an international nonprofit organization headquartered in Boerne, Texas, near San Antonio. He is author of seventeen books, including *The Superbeings, The Angels Within Us,* and *The Abundance Book.* He has been a keynote speaker at national conferences and, with his wife, Jan, conducts workshops in Raising Consciousness, Facing Change Creatively, The Secret of Success, Healing Relationships, Abundance, and The Wholeness Principle. He and Jan originated World Healing Day, which has taken place each year on December 31 since 1986. He is the recipient of several humanitarian awards, including the International New Thought Alliance's Joseph Murphy Award. A frequent guest on radio, he has appeared on the Wisdom Channel and major market television to talk about his books.

Part V
Spiritual Life

Introduction: A Universal Spirituality

Dr. Roger W. Teel

During the Vietnam War, a young Air Force captain and his squad jumped from a helicopter near Khe Sahn. Almost immediately, the captain saw a live grenade on the ground near his crew. Instinct prompted him to throw it out of harm's way, but as he took the grenade in his hand, it exploded, severing his right arm and both of his legs. Though the young soldier made a gradual physical recovery, spiritual healing came more slowly. Could he make peace with the experience and find the strength to trust life again? Could someone with just a left arm and a torso find life's meaning and vital purpose? Would he ever know true fulfillment?

Who doesn't entertain similar questions as life flows on? Yet, it's when we encounter life's "bombshell experiences" that the search intensifies. Perhaps this deeper searching is the real gift hidden in the toughest of times. One night in the hospital, the young captain had a spiritual experience. It was as though some higher power or greater intelligence was suffusing him with divine love. In that transcendent moment, a clear message burst forth within his awareness. He realized that his brains weren't in his legs or his arms, but in his head—and he still had that. He remembered that he had a sturdy heart, along with the ability and desire to believe in something greater than himself. That something, he knew, could help him renew his belief in himself and in his dreams and possibilities. The inward message concluded that he must never, ever give up—never, never, never!

Spiritual moments like this are transforming. They have come to people throughout history and across the wide spectrum of cultures and spiritual paths. Something in this universe is definitely "there" for us and seeks to evidence itself through us. It seems that anyone looking for spiritual development and empowerment needs only to seek sincerely in order to find them.

New Thought spirituality gleans the clearest insights from many spiritual paths, the ancient wisdom as well as modern inspiration, philosophy, and science. The resulting synthesis produces a *universal spirituality,* an expression of core principles and practices that heal, transform, and enrich lives. The inspirational articles in this section clarify and develop the principles and practices of New Thought spirituality. As an introduction, it may be helpful to look at some of the most common themes:

A Universal Presence

New Thought invites you to attune yourself to the Creative Source, God, Spirit, Infinite Life—whatever name you choose—not as a distant entity, but as a universal presence. The motivating energy of this presence is love. This presence is the ground of all being, the creator of all things visible and tangible. This presence of love births you and all things as divine ideas blessed with an inherently perfect pattern of being. All creation remains forever united with this presence, from which all life and sustenance are derived.

An Infinite Power

God—this ultimate, universal source—is experienced as an infinite, creative power as well as a universal presence of love. This power draws upon its infinite intelligence, options, and resources to bring creation into manifest form following Love's divine design. God, as infinite power, is a limitless force for Good; it is the power attendant to every prayer. As Dr. Ernest Holmes declared, "There is a Power for Good in this universe greater than we are, and we can use It."

A Transformed Identity

With the realization of God-Life as both universal presence and infinite power, it becomes clear that all life lives, moves, and has its being in this divine source. Moreover, New Thought teaches that love's divine design for every human being is to be made in the image and likeness of God, reproducing in microcosm what the Creator is in the macrocosm. Instead of seeing yourself as a separated, unworthy being, New Thought offers to everyone the healing experience of a transformed identity. Contemplate yourself as a spiritual and creative being forever loved and in unity with your source. Sense that your dreams are love's impulse for life within you!

A New Path

Bolstered by a transformed identity, New Thought teaches that each person is spiritually empowered to live a purposeful, productive, joyous, and evolving life. As centers of creative intelligence, it is "done unto us as we believe." New Thought teaches that anyone may birth a creative idea and set it in motion to become form by means of infinite power. Our highest path is to align our awareness with the presence and to cocreate with God the healing, blessing, and advancement of life on this planet.

How does such spirituality impact an individual human life? Return for a moment to that wounded Air Force captain. The power of his spiritual experience was obvious in the moment, yet he never could have imagined its long-term blessings and where the promptings of that inner voice would take him. The soldier's name is Max Cleland,

and the day would come when he would be wheeled into the Oval Office of the White House, administered an oath by the President, and named Administrator of the Department of Veterans Affairs. When his appointment came up for confirmation before the United States Senate, it received a cheering, standing ovation and passed without even one dissenting vote. Max Cleland has gone on to many other accomplishments, yet none of them would have been possible without his discovery of the comfort, support, and motivating love of Spirit!

Who knows what blessings are waiting to be poured into your experience through that same discovery? Welcome to your spirituality, to the path that leads to who you really are!

Spiritual Simplicity

Rev. Carol Carnes

True spirituality has always required that we balance the physical self, the body and personality, with the spiritual self, the inner spirit or soul. There's no denying that to get along in the world, we have to have a firm grounding in the physical, in the everyday reality of time and space. But we must not become mired in it. Our well-being also demands that we fulfill our souls' needs in ways that harmonize with our personalities. Ignore the needs of the soul and we risk becoming lost in the local. In the extreme, this imbalance may manifest as depression, mental dullness, exhaustion, or addiction. More commonly, we feel a conflict between our spiritual desire for love and our "need" to win, between our longing for solitude and our drive to achieve, between our love of community and our quest for power.

How, then, might we bridge that "gap" between spirit and ego, soul and personality, truth and facts, heaven and earth? Every generation assumes that it has the answer. In times past, we were admonished to follow strictly the rules of religion. "Learn the scriptures and live by them," we were advised, and our lives would find a natural balance.

Many of us who came to adulthood over the last several decades have tried more colorful remedies. In the 1960s, the cry was "Turn on, tune in, just drop out of this mechanistic, materialistic, plastic, and stressful society. Come and play in strawberry fields forever." That lifestyle got old quickly, not only because there were children to feed and clothe but also because the physical self needs to be productive. We have a built-in tendency to achieve, to make our mark, to excel at something.

By the time the seventies came around, we were at a loss, so we just gave up and gave in to a philosophy that can be summed up as "if it feels good, do it." In the eighties, we resolved anew to serve the physical self. We said, "to heck with the inner self" and turned our attention to producing and achieving with a vengeance! But ignoring Spirit completely gave us an ache in our collective psyche. Many of us noticed that the more successful we became, the busier we got. The more money we piled up and the more responsibilities we had, the more attractive the notion of running away from it all became! Life in a monastery started sounding good. Those who did drop out, on the other hand, who went off to India with just a spare pair of jeans, secretly longed to be rich, to shine, to be acknowledged for some accomplishment.

Now, at the opening of the twenty-first century, let's hope we have learned something from these experiments. The answer to the age-old conflict between the physical and spiritual may be just this: "Simplify." Many of us are finding that we don't really have to run off to the South Pacific to find peace and balance; nor are we required to give up our well-paying jobs to attend to Spirit. All that's required is that we take charge of our time and space and choose activities that feed the soul. The trick is finding ways to weave spirituality into our daily lives.

The soul craves beauty, order, solitude, love, play, community, creativity, and celebration. Fulfilling each of these needs in small ways takes only a little thought, but the benefits are stunning. As we make choices to feed the soul, we realize again that the good we seek is right where we are. As we bring the energies of spirit and body into balance, we unleash our creativity and find new outlets for expressing the soul's truth. As the physical self is healed of its quest for external power, the personality actually becomes a clearer vehicle for creative self-expression.

If this recipe for saner living sounds good to you, how might you begin? First, remember that to simplify also means to slow down. Start your day with quiet meditation or beautiful music. Sing in the shower; walk around the block and bring home fresh flowers. Doing these things takes no more time than you'd spend watching the news or reading the paper. But which activities feed the soul?

Next, resist the urge to accept every social invitation that comes your way. The soul craves solitude as well as company, and keeping company with the self can be great fun. I know a woman who takes her roller blades to the office and uses her lunch hour to glide solo around the neighborhood. Your need for community can be served by a "no TV" evening during which the family talks or plays games or sings together.

As you get into the habit of considering the needs of your spiritual self, you will think of many ways to serve them. Digging in the garden, baking bread or knitting a sweater, writing a poem or a letter, making a list of all the things for which you feel grateful—these are but a few of the many ways you can begin to move into a greater balance of spirit and body. Even cleaning out a closet fulfills the soul's desire for order, which may, in turn, clear the mental space through which creative ideas can come into expression.

Simplicity brings other gifts as well. As you consciously use your time to nourish the Spirit, you may find yourself responding to events from a centered place rather than reacting from fear. You may be more present in your relationships, clearer in your decision making, and better able to ask yourself before acting, "Does this serve my soul?"

Moreover, a simple and balanced life expands your awareness of the whole self within and the good that is now at hand. The quieter you become on the inside, the more naturally you respond to the inner impulses of Spirit, which seek expression through you. Perhaps the most fulfilling of these soul promptings is the impulse to love. When you move from an outer-directed life to one of spiritual simplicity, you come to know that the spiritual self is always poised to act with kindness and compassion, understanding and generosity. It is the personality that fears rejection and seeks to protect itself with false pride.

If there is one thing we have learned since the sixties, it's that we cannot solve our problems by running away from home. We are right where we need to be to discover who we are, and only from this discovery of our wholeness are things made new in this world. Spiritual maturity means spiritual simplicity. Each of us must build our own bridge to heaven. Doing so effectively brings heaven to earth.

CAROL CARNES is senior minister of the Center for Positive Living in Sarasota, Florida, having previously pastored New Thought churches in Tennessee and Calgary, Canada. She is known for her "cut to the chase" style of speaking and her playful presentations of ancient wisdom in modern language. She has served on the board of directors of Religious Science International and is currently a member of the Leadership Council of the Association for Global New Thought. She was a featured monthly writer for *Creative Thought Magazine* and has given keynotes and presentations at international conferences. She was recently inducted into the Martin Luther King Order of Preachers at Morehouse College.

Heaven on Earth

Rev. Rita Marie Johnson, Ph.D.,
and Rev. Juan Enrique Toro

In August 1999, Pope John Paul II concluded a twenty-two-day session of spiritual teaching with a monumental message to the world that stated the Vatican's new position about the afterlife. The Pope said that heaven, hell, and purgatory are not physical locations but experiences that reflect varying degrees of unity with God. In other words, heaven and hell are states of consciousness that result from our living, personal relationship with the divine.

Although I am no longer Catholic, I can imagine that this statement caused an earthquake in the thinking of Catholics around the world. I vividly remember the horrors of hell and purgatory as they were graphically and emphatically explained to me. My young head was filled with images of perpetual suffering and with the uncertain fate of countless souls trapped in the gray area of purgatory, not quite good enough to get into heaven but not bad enough for hell. Though I certainly feared the eternal flames and damnation that awaited the evil ones in hell, I was also repelled by the description of purgatory's perpetual waiting lounge for lost souls. The message to me was clear:

Fly right, be a good person, and you will avoid some terrible consequences after you die.

The Pope's recent message did away with all of that afterlife thinking. Moving beyond the conception of a literal heaven and hell, whether as a result of the Pope's words or of our own thoughts, represents such a radical change in the basic belief system of so many people that a few questions naturally come to mind:

1. Does taking away the threat of purgatory and hell eliminate the consequences of wrongdoing?
2. If there is no heaven, what motivates us to be good?
3. If heaven and hell are not physical locations, where are they?

New Thought has always embraced the idea that heaven and hell are states of consciousness. It reasons that no one needs to be reminded what hell feels like, since all of us have been there at some time or another in our lives and know its bite and remember its sting. We know hell as the darkness of deep depression, the stress of too many bills and too little money, the feeling of abandonment, abuse, or aggression.

The Pope suggested that we experience these emotions when we mistakenly try to separate ourselves from the eternal love that is God. As a consequence of this sense of separation, we make our lives "a living hell." In other words, we are responsible for our own hell experience—not in the way I was taught as a young Catholic, but by allowing a sense of separation from God to persist. Of course, if we are responsible for creating the problem of hell consciousness, we can also be part of the solution. Put in simple terms, if hell is separation from God, then heaven is conscious union with the divine.

If the reward of heavenly bliss is also a state of mind, then what motivates us to be good? Our own experiences teach us the answer to this question as well. We know that life is more positive and more fulfilling when we contemplate beauty, when we express love, gratitude, and compassion. Perhaps this positive state of being is heaven on earth, the unity consciousness that has been the experience of mystics and saints throughout history.

The bottom line on this new way of thinking is that we can create the experiences of heaven and hell consciousness right here and right now. Goodness and grace are our birthright, the gifts of an unconditionally loving God. We can choose, on a daily basis, greater or lesser expressions of these blessings. When we consciously join with God and allow the divine to express in and through us as love, life, and peace, we are truly in heaven.

Beyond challenging people to seek greater understanding of age-old ideas, the Pope's 1999 message also pushed the world a step closer to global unity. By shifting the attention of people around the world from an emphasis on the afterlife to their present experience of God, the hearts and minds of people all over the planet were joined, for the experience of heaven and hell, right here on earth, is both personal and universal.

The awareness of God's presence is beyond words, yet it is so powerful and beautiful that the human soul is compelled to describe to others what it feels like to touch the divine. But when we try to explain this experience, differences often arise that seem to separate us and often lead to disagreements and even to wars.

Yet the experience of God prevails as a common thread for all humanity. We can celebrate our own, and our brothers' and sisters', experience of God by knowing that beyond the words, beyond the theology and practice of our particular brand of spirituality, is a marvelous unity. Then we realize that what is pure and sacred about our personal experience with God is true for believers everywhere.

We are moving, step by step, toward a worldwide focus on an experience of God that joins us rather than on the theological explanations of religion that sometimes separate us. The declarations of Pope John Paul II regarding heaven and hell were a giant step in this direction, as they emphasized spiritual experience rather than religious dogma.

In the coming years, religious leaders from around the world will be meeting through various venues to focus on their commonality and, on that basis, to search for ways to end religious wars. These dialogues are an important aspect of the move away from dogma and toward an experience of oneness. What if the world's religious leaders could rally around a statement such as this?

We are willing to see beyond our theological differences and to recognize that the experience of the love of God is common to all human beings. This experience joins us, heals all hurt, and gives us the wisdom to create a world where we can live together in peace.

I can accept and hold this truth in my heart, and I believe our religious leaders can, too. As we all claim this simple idea, the pain of conflict over religious differences will be transcended, freeing us to create heaven on earth.

Heaven on earth! Now there's an idea we can all agree on.

RITA MARIE JOHNSON is founder and director of the Rasur Foundation for Wisdom Education in Costa Rica, an international organization that works to bring spiritual principles into education. She has been an instructor at the University of Texas and Austin Community College. An ordained Unity minister, she has pioneered churches in Puerto Rico and, with her husband, Juan Enrique Toro, in Costa Rica.

JUAN ENRIQUE TORO, also an ordained Unity minister, is the leader of Unity-Costa Rica. His radio messages are heard throughout Costa Rica, and his programs for Radio for Peace International are broadcast around the world. He served on the international task force for "A Season for Nonviolence" and gives workshops in many Latin American countries, including Colombia, Santa Domingo, Mexico, and Cuba.

Empower the Flower

David Leonard

I am a gardener, both physically and spiritually. In my relationships with plants, I see the miracle of life emerge in all its mysterious magnificence. Ralph Waldo Emerson sings in my soul, "What is nature but a mute gospel . . . the very earth laughs in flowers." Something in me smiles as I breathe in these ideas.

Adam and Eve were given one task, to tend the garden. Could I honor that simple challenge within myself and my world and make it bloom? Could I be like one of the lilies of the field and not struggle, but unfold in my own unique way with ease and joy?

Ernest Holmes reminds us that "inherent in the seed is the flower." I have to ask myself then, "What seeds am I watering within the soil of my consciousness?" If they are seeds of enlightenment, peace, and soulful awareness, then that is what will grow; but if they are seeds of doubt, fear, and worry, so will grow my inner garden. I hold the watering can with my conscious attention. How glorious to know that I can empower the flower of my choice by watering the seeds within, realizing that they will bloom in their right and perfect time. Your life, too, will bloom when it is ready!

Dr. Holmes goes on to say, "We need not coerce, we do not create the power, but must LET this Great Power operate through us. There should not be any sense of hurry or worry about this, just a calm, peaceful sense of reality. There should be no idea of compulsion."[1] This is a lesson we have to learn for ourselves.

Years ago I was given an orchid as a gift. Such an exotic-looking thing! The very thought of its blooming excited me. I did my best to provide the plant with the right environment: proper watering, fertilizer, great light, knowing that when it was ready, it would present me an incredible flower as the reward for my service.

Six months passed, and the plant just seemed to stand still, showing no new growth. When I had given up hope of ever seeing a bloom, I noticed that the orchid had some new sprouts and that they contained within them the beginnings of a spindly protuberance, which I grasped must be the blossom to be. Weeks passed as the plant gradually sent up a long spike that ultimately revealed three buds. Each day I went to it and affirmed its beauty and its special place in my heart.

Yes, I talk to plants. The world may call me crazy, but that's the way I am. All life responds to love and tenderness, and plants are no different. So, I found myself being a cheerleader for this strange orchid in my sunny east window. Every morning I would whisper, "You look marvelous, darling! I know you can do it! We're all so excited to see you do your thing!"

As time dragged on I found myself mumbling, "Hurry up already! How long is this going to take? I haven't got two lifetimes, you know!" Clearly, I was not in that place of "smiling repose" that Emerson extols. If it is the "little self that wails and suffers," I must have been slipping into my little self by leaps and bounds. I had become the anxious kid who couldn't wait any longer.

Eventually the buds had swollen so that the outline of the petals appeared. They seemed to be a reddish-purple. Oh, the anticipation was torturing me! What would the demonstration of my devotion

---

[1] Holmes, Ernest, *The Science of Mind* (New York: G. P. Putnam's Sons, 1938), 140.

look like? Daily I would go to the plant, stare at those swollen buds, and wonder when they would open. Out of frustration, I turned my inspection tour into a sacred ritual. I would do my morning meditation focusing on the plant, as the east light shone on the swollen buds, desiring to be there in that moment of moments when the petals would finally unfurl. But no matter how hard I wished for it, the miracle didn't happen.

Just as the watched pot never boils, neither does the reluctant orchid willingly open. One morning something snapped in my brain. It was as if I had become a mad scientist and had had enough of the waiting. I found myself rummaging through the kitchen drawer for a knife that could loosen those stubborn lavender petals so I could have my long-awaited reward.

I know it sounds sick. It was. I had become obsessed with the mystery bloom and had decided that I was going to have it now. I must apologize to the plant for my overzealous fervor that mutilated that first bloom. I did, however, learn an invaluable lesson.

You cannot coerce a demonstration to happen any faster than it wants to. Lord Buddha said, and I'm paraphrasing, "When conditions are right, things manifest, and when they are not right, they don't." A butterfly takes time to form within the cocoon before it can emerge. The chick takes time before it is ready to hatch, and you and I must be patient as we allow for our own metamorphosis or blossoming.

A little plant showed me my own impatience with natural process. When conditions are right, things bloom, and it is counterproductive to force the issue. The sun is going to rise at the right time, and our lives will unfold when we are ripe.

It took Moses forty years to get out of Egypt. He had to be willing to leave an outmoded idea of himself and to embark on an unknown life in Midian. It took forty more years before he heard the voice of God speak to him and tell him to free his people. Then forty more years had to pass in the wilderness before some were permitted to enter the Promised Land. Forty years, it seems, represents the time it takes something to come to fruition. Get it?

It is worthy to note that Moses did not enter the Promised Land, because, like me with that orchid bloom, he didn't have the patience to wait upon the Lord. The Lord represents the Law, as we learn in New Thought, "We do not make the Law work; it is its nature to work." And it is our job to be patient and let it.

As conscious expressions of life, we bloom in the moment by courting the presence within us and waiting for the law of unfoldment to fulfill itself. We *are* like the lilies of the field, and when we trust in the flow, we grow into greater ideas that emerge naturally as our lives blossom.

Today we witness the flowers that are a result of the seeds we have watered in consciousness. Tomorrow will produce new growth, new buds, and different flowers. Our task is to tend the gardens of our souls, observe the swelling buds, and wait patiently for them to open. The blooming gardens that result are our juicy lives emerging in beauty and wonder, as exotic as the rarest flower.

Let us know that we demonstrate heaven on earth when we let heaven blossom in our hearts. We can't force the dawn, and we can't coerce the demonstration of our lives or anybody else's life. We can, however, rest in smiling repose and trust in the Law to do what it does through us in the perfect time. Like the lily, we do not toil, neither do we struggle, yet Solomon in all his splendor is not arrayed like one of these.

Empower the flowers inherent within the gardens of our souls, trusting that our lives blossom when we are ready. How sweet it is! As the Zen poet Basho reminds us:

> The temple bell stops
> But the sound keeps coming out of the flowers.

DAVID LEONARD is the pastor of the Center for Conscious Living in Hunstville, Alabama. His ministry is characterized by creative soulful expression. His stage background helps him liberate the authentic self through "Soul Dancing." He tends gardens within and without and feels his purpose is to help others bloom to their full divine potential. A frequent speaker at New Thought events, he also conducts transformational seminars.

Feeding the White Dog

Kathy Gottberg

The late Joseph Campbell once told friends that he was raised to believe literally that a tiny angel sat on one of his shoulders and a tiny devil on the other. Though he outgrew that idea, he acknowledged that we all embody and reflect opposing forces of light and dark. A Native American medicine man described the same opposition in a different way. He said that each person contains both a white dog and a black dog. The white dog represents our highest possibility, unconditional love, and our spirit in action. The black dog is ignorance, judgment, and fear. These two dogs, the medicine man explained, are in a constant battle. When a young boy asked the medicine man which dog wins, the medicine man answered, "The dog I feed."

Which dog do you feed? That is a question I've been asking myself lately. Any time I participate in a conversation that promotes fear, judgment, or prejudice, I am feeding the black dog. Any time I watch the news on television and repeat the terror, any time I share information about someone when I don't really know the truth, any time I make others wrong in order to make myself feel right—I'm feeding the black dog.

Feeding the white dog seems easy. All it takes is remembering to live in the light. All it takes is a recognition that life is whole, interconnected, and deeply loving. But, even though that prescription sounds simple and positive, staying focused on the white dog, as most of us know, is sometimes a challenge. Why is this so?

I recently read the book *Letters to Vanessa, On Love, Science and Awareness in an Enchanted World* by Jeremy W. Hayward.[1] Hayward suggests that we don't live in an "enchanted world" because we choose to live in what he calls "dead world." Dead world is the mechanistic, linear, and materialistic worldview that is insidiously prevalent to most of us as the true "reality." Hayward reminds us that this "dead" way of looking at our world is a lie. The world is actually vibrantly alive, interconnected, and suffused with possibility. It is only by habit that we see it as limited and inert. Let me give you an example.

Several hundred years ago Isaac Newton began developing mechanical laws to explain the forces of nature. In order to explain his famous law of motion, he had to imagine a couple of things. He had to imagine that there was a fixed background for everything that was empty, passive, and not affected by anything else. He called that fixed background "absolute space." He also had to imagine that there was universal time that existed on all planets equally and that was also not connected to or affected by anything else. He called this construct "absolute time." Now, remember, Newton made up these two absolutes! Absolute time and absolute space are only hypotheses.

Unfortunately, the world became so enamored of Newton's laws that we now consider absolute time and absolute space to be *real*. Somewhere along the line we forgot that time is nothing more than a measurement of change. We also forgot that space is pliable. Even scientists like Einstein and the current crop of quantum thinkers, who have long since proven that time and space are relative and flexible, have not convinced us to give up the mechanical, materialistic, dead world view of time and space.

[1] Jeremy W. Hayward, *Letters to Vanessa, On Love, Science and Awareness in an Enchanted World* (Boston: Shambhala, 1997).

Some of the evidence that Jeremy Hayward uses in his book to remind us that we inhabit a living, conscious universe rather than a dead world is intriguing. He cites, for instance, the experiments held at PEAR (Princeton Engineering Anomalies Research) during the last fifteen years. The most remarkable results have come from a machine called the REG (random event generator). This electronic machine is designed to demonstrate the equivalent of tossing a coin and counting heads and tails. Normally, if you toss a coin 100 times, you'd expect to get approximately 50 heads and 50 tails. The REG uses "zeros" and "ones." Approximately fifty percent of the time, as you'd expect, the REG produces zeros; the other fifty percent, it produces ones.

Here's how the experiments worked. A person was placed in the room with the REG and asked to "influence" it so that it produced more zeros or more ones than it would if left alone. Over 597 experiments were done using 68 people. Amazingly, the experiments showed that people had a remarkable ability to affect the outcome of the electronic "coin toss." According to Hayward, "It has been estimated that when the results of all these studies are included, the odds against chance being the explanation for them are 1 in 10^{35} (that means 1 followed by 35 zeros)." In other words, these experiments showed that the thoughts and intentions of the human mind do affect things—machines like cars and computers, other people, and yes, even ourselves.

Moreover, the REG experiments showed dramatically that mind can affect matter over a distance. Research subjects were asked to try to influence the machine from hundreds of miles away. Results showed that these attempts were just as successful as if the person "sending" the thoughts was in the same room as the machine. Given these findings, can you have any doubt that the most powerful kind of thought or intention we send, prayer, can influence "reality"?

Other REG experiments found that pairs of men and women had significantly more influence over the machine when they worked together. Beyond that, they found that any bonded or committed pair of people had as much as seven times greater influence than an individual working alone. Finally, they showed that men and women produced different responses. Women produced a greater effect when they produced one, while men proved to be more consistent overall in influencing the machine.

What are the implications of these experiments for our spiritual lives? First, I think it is important to note that while people had a definite, irrefutable influence on "reality," they were not able to transform it completely by making the machine produce, say, all zeros or all ones. Instead the influence of mind over matter is only partial. So, as other experiments showed, it makes sense that we maximize our ability to influence the world by coming together with focus and intention in a group. In other words, the undeniable power of personal prayer is multiplied in the associations we form and the people with whom we surround ourselves. Influencing "reality" takes all of us!

Though Joseph Campbell's twin angels may be an oversimplification, it also seems clear that we have a choice. We can go on acting as if Newton's static and linear world of absolute space and absolute time is real. Or, we can fight against that limiting perception and accept, using, if we need to, the ammunition of contemporary experimental science, to prove to ourselves that the world we inhabit is vibrantly alive and interconnected. Space does not stop with me and begin with you. If we are truly One, and our thoughts affect one another, all the thoughts I have and all the thoughts you have affect every person and every thing on the planet.

We even affect the earth herself. If I think of our planet as a dead world, a machine that is separate from myself that is getting old and running down, I'm contributing to the earth's destruction. If I act out of fear, competition, and judgment as though I alone matter, I help create a dead world. However, if I remember that what I do to another person and what I do to the planet, I do to myself, then I am helping to heal the earth. When we speak of wholeness, love, and possibility, we promote the light.

That's where the white dog comes in. The white dog is the light in ourselves and in the universe. It is waiting for us to "feed it" by our thoughts, intentions, and actions. Every moment of every day we choose which dog we will feed. Feed the white dog. With everyone's help, it wins!

The Bible, Our Spiritual Evolution

Debra Ann Dixon

Sometimes people think that in New Thought, the Bible has become obsolete. This simply is not true. In Unity, for instance, we use the Bible as our major textbook. We see it as a rich metaphysical reference that is alive and relevant to us today. As an example, I often think of my own spiritual journey using a biblical framework. In sharing how the Bible has helped me to understand the events of my life, I am inviting you to seek guidance about your own story as you read and study the Bible's characters and events.

For me, the Bible has become a metaphor for my life experience. Like the Hebrew people, I have been released from bondage in the land of Egypt and led through the wilderness into the Promised Land. I have suffered my own Babylonian exile. I have been the repentant John the Baptist awaiting and preparing for the Christ. The passion of Jesus has given me insight into my own crucifixions and has pointed me toward my resurrection and second coming.

At the time of my most profound bondage to an outmoded belief system, I was living in a convent. In my struggles, I remember praying for deliverance. Asking God for direction, I opened my Bible at random to a verse from Jeremiah: "Set up signposts. Raise landmarks, mark the road well by which you went. Come home virgin of Israel. Come home to these towns of yours. For Yahweh is creating something new on earth and the woman sets out to find her husband again" (Jer. 31:21).

Since I did not immediately understand the meaning of that reading, I asked for another. This time I opened the Bible to Hosea: "And that is why I am going to lure her and lead her out into the wilderness and speak to her heart. I am going to give her back her vineyards and I am going to make the Valley of Achor a gateway of hope. And there she will respond to me like when she was young. And when that day comes she will no longer call me my Baal but my Husband" (Hosea 2: 16–18).

It has taken me years to understand the full significance of these two passages. I now see that God was telling me to "come home" to myself, to lay claim to the richness of my life in Spirit. Divine Spirit would then give me my "vineyards"—my divine inheritance. God was asking me to go "out into the wilderness," to visit the unexplored parts of myself. I was to "mark the road well" by examining my life and by remembering where I came from, taking the good and leaving the rest. I was to see that all the parts of my life work together for my good and that all things are in divine order.

In Hebrew, the "Valley of Achor" means a place of misfortune or despair. These passages promised that all of my despair would turn into a gateway of hope. The divine light of understanding would dissolve the shadows because Yahweh would show me "something new on earth." In other words, God was calling me to walk a new path and to be born again. To create my new life, I was to let go of my narrow consciousness so that I could move into an expanded view of myself and the world. Then, the text says, "the woman sets out to find her husband again." The word "husband" here stands for personal and spiritual fulfillment.

I have come to understand that my spiritual journey was not supposed to end in the convent, but to begin there. The constraints of formal religion were my stepping stone to becoming a more spiritual person, one who would be prepared to do the hard internal work of becoming conscious of the Christ within. God was inviting me to walk closer to him, but the tone of my relationship needed to change: "And in that day she will no longer call me my Baal but my Husband." The word "Baal" means "master." I was being told that my relationship to God should no longer be that of a servant to her master, but a deeper and more loving bond, like that of a wife to her husband: "And the two shall become one."

In her *Healing Letters,* Myrtle Fillmore affirmed that her higher qualities were also being unified with the divine. She wrote, "My faith, understanding, and love are now becoming one." I began to recognize that I, too, was being invited to participate in a mystical marriage. I began to understand the deeper meaning of other passages of Scripture: "The Father and I are one" (John 10:30) and, "What therefore God hath joined together let not man put asunder" (Matt. 19:6). Once I realized that God is the fountain from which all my good would spring, nothing that anyone did, said, or failed to do could take away my joy and my good.

The Unity movement was my Promised Land of freedom, where perfect love and goodness reign. Once I entered, there was no turning back. Through the application of Unity principles, I could understand the metaphysical meaning of these Bible verses, and my life was forever changed. Though entering into the Promised Land of Unity and New Thought was a new beginning for my evolving consciousness, I still had my battles to fight.

The most fearsome adversary I had to face was my own addictions. I like to describe the state of being addicted as my "exile in Babylon." Babylon represents any confused state of consciousness in the material world. In essence, I had fallen victim to thinking that my suffering was the result of things outside myself. I felt justified in my anger at my many disappointments and fell into the trap of believing that I could end my suffering from the outside in by overindulging in the physical world and its temptations.

But as many of us who have experienced the Babylonian exile of addiction know, eventually there comes a hunger. I hungered for the restoration experience of "remembering the Father's house." I remembered the "vineyards" that God had promised me. The healing thought that I would be warmly welcomed when I returned from exile helped me to overcome my addictions and to find my vocation as a holistic healer and Unity spiritual teacher and leader.

When I understood the work I was to do, I entered into the intellectual state of John the Baptist. Metaphysically, John represents the intellect. Preparing the mind is the first step of entering into Christ consciousness. But I had to be wary of the pitfall of getting so involved in the "intellectual" image of what I should do that I would never allow the idea to manifest in my life. The proper use of the intellect, as the law of mind action teaches us, is to prepare the way for the good to manifest in our lives by creating appropriate thoughts. As we prepare our minds to receive the Christ through understanding spiritual principles, the ground of life is prepared for our ideas to grow and flower.

The idea I planted in the ground of my own consciousness was the image of myself as planter of seeds in others. In my work, I aspire to nurture seeds of faith by recognizing the Christ potential in each person. Being so seen enables others to realize their connection with their inner power. I feel called to inspire insight that activates the inner wisdom we all possess, and I strive to give loving support to the healing potential that is our birthright.

In coming back to myself, I entered into the deeper awareness of knowing that all my crucifixions—my disappointments, pains, and even deaths—have been part of my creative process. The more fully I live my sorrows as well as celebrate my joys, the more I experience the all-ness of life. I no longer run from pain. I understand that life is full of disappointments and injustices, but I am charged with new perspective. I do not judge by appearances; my understanding faith tells me that all things can lead to my good.

When we go with the flow of life, a resurrection happens in us. Jesus said to the man with the withered hand, "Stretch forth thy hand." That Christ Spirit is offering us the opportunity to stretch beyond the withered part of us—our limited thinking. Stretch beyond the appearances of lack, limitation, and pain, and reconnect through prayer and meditation to our indwelling Christ. When we affirm that there is only one presence and one power operating in all of life, we experience the second coming of moving beyond any sense of separation between God and humankind.

As Charles Fillmore tells us in *The Revealing Word:* "The second coming is the result of building the principles of Being into the soul of man, where they begin to express through him." Though the Father does the work, I have come to understand that the Christ experience happens through us. The Bible can be our guide and counselor during that sacred process.

DEBRA ANN DIXON is a licensed Unity teacher and spiritual leader of Unity Church of Crystal Lake in Crystal Lake, Illinois. She is a highly trained practitioner in many areas of holistic health care, including massage therapy, reflexology, Reiki, herbal therapy, hypnotherapy, and body-centered psychotherapy, with an ongoing private practice.

The Transformation of
Robben Island

Rev. Dr. Christian Sorensen

Most countries have their own Alcatraz, a maximum security prison in an escape-proof location to which the so-called unwanted of society can be banished. South Africa is no different. It had Robben Island, a rock eleven miles off Cape Town jutting out into the middle of Table Bay. When apartheid ended, an amazing transformation took place at Robben Island. Its political prisoners, those who had challenged the evils of apartheid, were released, and the island was opened for all people to visit.

At the close of the millennium, Robben Island received recognition as a World Heritage site. That same week, a delegation from the Parliament of the World's Religions taking place in Cape Town took an early morning ferry out to the island to plant a peace pole. Some 200,000 of these poles have been planted around the globe. Each is inscribed with the words "May Peace Prevail on Earth." The pole planted on Robben Island carries this message not only in English but also in Zulu, Xhosa, and Afrikaans. Participants at the ceremony on Robben Island stood beneath the flags of 185 nations from around the world. We were moved to tears when the Isibane youth choir sang: "Africa, it's been so long killing each other" and "Can you understand how I suffer?"

To appreciate the impact of this moment, you need to know a bit of the history of Robben Island. In its prison past, Robben Island was a place of profound inhumanity—regular beatings, dog attacks, and the horrific caging of human beings. Men were forced to crush stone in the lime quarries to try to quash their spirits for having spoken out against the injustices of apartheid. When they were released from prison, these men had every reason to be filled with hatred, anger, bitterness, and rage, yet something entirely different took place. Many of the men imprisoned on Robben Island had used their solitary time there to better themselves, including some who had been imprisoned for more than a quarter of a century. Their spirit turned a "nightmare" hell into an historic educational opportunity. So, when the cell doors finally opened, they stepped forth not only as heroes but also as leaders.

Among them was Nelson Mandela. He stepped forth to become the president of South Africa, taking power through a peaceful revolution that stunned the world. He told our group: "While we would not want to forget the brutality of apartheid, what we want to reflect upon is the triumph of the human spirit against the forces of evil."

Remembering these words and the undeniable power of Robben Island as a symbol leads me to ask: Where in your life have you been imprisoned? In what hell of your own creation have you found yourself trapped? What seemingly hopeless situation in your life begs for transformation?

All too often, we imprison ourselves by the concepts we accept as true, including our conception of God. Among these constricting concepts is the belief that our comfort depends on external conditions, rather than on what's going on inside. Thus, when our comfortable existence is shaken to the core, we have nothing on which to rely. A true spiritual life reverses this dynamic. It suggests that, even when the world outside has become a nightmare place of suffering, we have the power to transform our hell into an opportunity for empowerment and growth.

When we feel imprisoned by sickness, lack, or limitation, we give our potential away to some physical condition, erroneously believing that something else is stronger than God. Whatever healing we need must be discovered within our own consciousness. Whether we find ourselves in a prison cell, or whether, as is more likely, we lose our job or face a financial challenge or a dissolving relationship, we can turn within to God for guidance, direction, and answers. The real substance of all form is invisible. All outer conditions are the result of inner activity.

When you are faced with a set of difficult circumstances, call to mind the picture of the peace pole at Robben Island. Use this image to remind yourself that all that is required to live life fully and effortlessly unfolds from within. Remind yourself that when you allow your trust, faith, and confidence to rest in God, and not in the outer conditions of the world, any circumstance, even the most difficult, can be transformed. It is God's good pleasure to give you the Kingdom, so let it be your good pleasure to receive it. When this belief becomes your persistent mental practice, you'll come to know that everything necessary to your freedom is already within you. Then, you, too, step out of prison a spiritual hero.

CHRISTIAN SORENSEN is senior minister of the Seaside Church of Religious Science in Encinitas, California, and president of the worldwide United Church of Religious Science. An avid sportsman, surfer, skier, and aviator, he has guided spiritual treks through the Himalayas, Russia, China, India, North Africa, Europe, Scandinavia, and the Mediterranean. He was host of the television program *Winds from the Sea* and is author of *Catch the Spirit: Riding the Waves of Life* and *Catch the Spirit: Flying Through Life*. A frequent speaker for spiritual, business, and social groups, he lights up his audiences with his expansive vision and enthusiasm.

Inside Prison Walls

Rev. Jane Drotar

In the last twenty-four years of my life, I have been outside these prison walls for a total of nine months." I sat startled as I listened to the middle-aged, bespeckled man in front of me. He could have passed for a high school teacher. "I am a junkie," he went on, "and everything everyone has ever said about me is true." He slumped back in his seat.

I was at a medium-security prison, involved in a volunteer program working with the inmates. I was helping to facilitate a discussion group that included about a dozen men who were serving sentences of under two years. The program enabled the men to discuss their feelings with one another in a safe environment.

The man sitting next to the first speaker now spoke up. "When I was eighteen years old," he began, "a drunk driver killed my twin sister." His voice cracked with emotion as he blinked back the tears. "Even now, her death breaks me up. She was my life.

"I despised the man who was driving the car that hit her. He was a former friend of mine. From that day on, my life was in a downward spiral. I ended up drinking and driving, and I killed someone myself as a drunk driver."

The man's final words were a revelation to me: "That which I despised for so long, I became!"

That which we despise, we become! The leader of the discussion group picked up on this thread immediately. "How many of you said you would never be like your father?"

To a man, the inmates raised their hands.

"How many of you are exactly like your father?"

Every hand remained in the air.

Resentment, holding on to anger—this is what imprisons us in life. These men were really in prison, but I wondered at that moment how many of the rest of us imprison ourselves with our resentments and our grudges. The Buddha described resentment as "picking up a hot coal to throw at someone." Of course, the person who picks up the coal is the one whose hand is burned first.

Here's an experiment you can try to see what a burden resentment can be. For each person against whom you hold a grudge, put a large raw potato into a bag. Carry that bag around with you everywhere you go. It doesn't take long for you to realize that carrying all that weight gets in your way. Through the freedom of forgiveness, we can lay down that burden and open the prison door.

The weight of the "story" we carry around with us saps our energy. And, while we are holding a grudge and feeling bitterness toward someone, that person may well be out dancing! Acid destroys the vessel in which it is held. Similarly, our unresolved resentments eat away at us and cause us many problems, physical as well as emotional.

Unity minister Catherine Ponder tells us that "unforgiveness blooms as debts" in our lives. When we are struggling and experiencing many problems, it may be time for us to stop and look at what debts we owe that can be paid off with forgiveness. Often, we find, what's really needed is for us to forgive ourselves.

That night at the prison, I shared a story with the inmates. I had been carrying around a feeling of resentment for a long time, I told them, and it had caused me great harm. While attending a seminar on forgiveness, I continued, I decided that it was time for me to let go of the situation and let the person toward whom I had been feeling resentment "off the hook."

The leader of the forgiveness seminar had suggested an exercise in releasing resentment. She warned us of the consequences. "Be very sure you are ready to let your feelings go, because after you have forgiven someone, you can no longer bring up 'the story.' You can no longer 'return to the scene of the crime.'"

Hearing those words, I told the inmates, had made me do some real soul searching. Was I really ready to let go of my resentment? Was I truthfully able to forgive and get on with my life? I took a deep breath and answered, "Yes." I said yes to Spirit. I was ready, and I knew that with the power of God within me, I could do it.

Jesus taught us the power of forgiveness. As it is used in the Bible, the word "forgive," in ancient Aramaic, the language Jesus is said to have spoken, means "to untie." When we refuse to forgive someone, we remain tied to them as surely as if we were being held in shackles. When an event from the past continually brings up resentment within us, we are stuck there, and we cannot move forward in life. We become immobilized.

In the Book of Mark, we find the story of the paralyzed man who was brought to Jesus. Four people carried the man on his bed. Since they could not get through the crowd surrounding Jesus, they lowered the man and his bed through the roof. Jesus told the man that his sins were forgiven. When those words caused a stir in the crowd, Jesus said, "Which is easier, to say . . . 'Your sins are forgiven' or to say 'Stand up and take your mat and walk'?" (Mark 2:9) Immediately, the man took his mat and walked!

Have you ever found yourself similarly paralyzed? Unable to move ahead? When you are in that state, if you turn to the Christ within you for help, the divine presence has the power to "forgive the sin." *Sin* simply means "error," getting off course. It is an archery term that means "missing the mark." If we stay in a place of unforgiveness, we miss the mark and stay stuck where we are. Forgiveness opens the door to movement. We "take our mat and walk," actually transcending what is binding us.

The moment I decided truly to forgive, I told the inmates, it was as if a harness had been taken off my shoulders. I felt the power of Spirit as it moved through me and broke the chains. What freedom! I had walked out of the prison gates of my unforgiveness and started moving again in my life.

Telling my story to the inmates and hearing theirs taught me a great lesson. We do become what we despise. I looked around that room and saw twelve human beings who had made mistakes, just as we all do. I saw their pain and torment as they recounted their difficulties and their early struggles, and I saw the promise of freedom for each one of them as they took responsibility for their actions and began the process of forgiveness.

JANE DROTAR is minister of Christ Church Unity in Hamilton, Ontario, Canada. As the Uniteens Consultant for the Eastern region of the Association of Unity Churches, she facilitated seminars and conferences for youth spiritual educators. A dynamic speaker, she has appeared in the "Positive Living Series" of motivational seminars and leads workshops in human development and potential.